Help!

I Can't Pay My Bills

Help!

I Can't Pay My Bills

Surviving a Financial Crisis

Sally Herigstad, C.P.A.

St. Martin's Griffin ⚏ New York

www.stmartins.com

Book design by rlf design

Library of Congress Cataloging-in-Publication Data

Herigstad, Sally.
    Help! I can't pay my bills : surviving a financial crisis / Sally Herigstad.
        p. cm.
    ISBN-13: 978-0-312-35928-7
    ISBN-10: 0-312-35928-4
    1. Finance, Personal. 2. Consumer credit. 3. Debt. I. Title.

  HG179.H447 2007
  332.024'02—dc22
                                                        2006050619

10 9 8 7 6 5 4 3

To my mother, Helen Lickey,

who knows how to stretch a dollar further

and with more style than anyone else I know.

No one has taught me more about managing

money than you, Mom.

Contents

Step Three

Make the Best Use of Your Money

Acknowledgments

I would especially like to thank the following people: Ted Weinstein, my agent, who understood from the beginning what I want to accomplish with this book; Ethan Friedman and Sheila Curry Oakes, my editors at St. Martin's Press; Craig Anderson, Helen Lickey, and Valia Sheidler, who read my rough draft and made suggestions that saved me from making a fool of myself; and, of course, my husband, Gary. Everything Gary or I do somehow ends up being a joint venture, and this book was no exception.

Step One

Face the Facts

1 How Did We Get Here?

Twenty-five years later, I still remember the day I got my first call from a collection department. I was a young stay-at-home mom. Our income had gone from sporadic to almost nonexistent in the recession of the early '80s, and the bills were piling up. By the time any money came in, it was spoken for many times over. I made a little cash watching two other babies along with my daughter. If I went to the grocery store with a twenty-dollar bill from babysitting, I thought I was really flush. I dreamed of being so rich someday that I could go to the grocery store any day of the month.

When the phone rang that day, it was a collections officer of a national department store. She asked me why we hadn't paid our bill. I told her that the construction business was slow right now. "It's been slow for a long time," she scolded. "Why did you buy things you knew you couldn't pay for?"

She went on, asking me what I had bought and reacting with scorn to each revelation. When she found out that I wasn't working full-time, she wanted to know why. The fact that I had a baby was to her just more evidence of my irresponsibility.

Trying to be cooperative, I answered all her probing, personal questions. When she had ridiculed me enough, she hung up. I had never felt so humiliated. I didn't think of myself as poor—I just didn't have any money right now. I lay across my bed and cried, wondering how it got this bad.

Unfortunately, that phone call was only the beginning. In the following months, I learned to dread answering the phone. I left stacks of mail unopened. I had a nervous feeling in the pit of my stomach all the time. I promised myself that I would never again complain about having bills to pay, if only I had the money to pay them with.

I wish I had known then what I know now. I felt alone with this embarrassing problem, and I couldn't see a way out of it. Nobody told me how many other people find themselves in the same predicament, let alone how anyone manages to cope and get through such a situation. In my fear, humiliation, and hopelessness, I felt trapped.

Eventually, I learned some lessons about managing money, and things began to slowly improve. We moved across the country for a steady job, and I was able to finish my college degree. We made a financial plan, and we paid off our debts. Nowadays when the phone rings, it's probably a friend. I am rich by the standards I set back then: I can buy groceries any day of the month! Still, I haven't forgotten how it felt to have bills I couldn't pay.

Unbeknown to me, I had plenty of company in the hard times. The average American family owes over $8,000 in credit card debt, and the national savings rate was *negative* in 2005. Over a million and a half Americans declare bankruptcy every year,* and many more are struggling to survive from day to day. One of the following circumstances is enough to cause a financial crisis—and a combination of two or more can be disastrous:

- **Divorce.** Some experts say that family breakups are the number one cause of poverty in America today. It's hard enough for two people to raise a family. A suddenly single parent can find the job overwhelming.

- **Catastrophic accidents or illness.** Medical bills not covered by insurance can devastate a family's finances. Even good health insurance may not cover all the expenses of a serious illness,

---

*SOURCE: http://www.uscourts.gov/bnkrpctystats/bankruptcystats.htm

such as travel and time off work for family members. Families reeling from a tragic accident or illness can find themselves facing medical bills and expenses larger than their annual income.

- **Unemployment.** Losing a job can mean suddenly facing a frightening new world with no regular paycheck. Unemployment compensation doesn't go far, and in a few weeks or months, families can get far behind in their bills.

- **Overspending.** Some people shop their way into a financial crisis. You don't have to be a compulsive spender to be shocked at how fast your money goes—or how quickly the debt adds up on your credit card bill. Without a good plan, you can spend more money than you should, even when you think you're being careful. Or an overspending spouse or other family member can do it for you.

- **Inexperience and lack of financial education.** As one young person said, "Why do they teach us calculus, but not things we really need to know about, like money?" Even a college degree is no guarantee that a person understands the basics of managing money. Young people who have recently moved away from the safety of their parents' homes can quickly get into more debt than they can handle. In fact, intelligent, responsible people of any age can make a few bad financial decisions and find themselves in trouble.

Why do we feel so alone when we have financial problems? People are expert at hiding their financial woes. You can't tell if they're having money problems by how they look. Sometimes the people in the most trouble are wearing the nicest clothes, or even driving the newest cars. They'll tell their friends about other personal problems, like how much weight they've gained, what the doctor said, and their last big fight at work. But their really big secret, the one that gnaws away at their insides all day and makes them eat too much and snap at family members, is too embarrassing to share.

Maybe if we were all more honest about our financial mistakes and problems, we could help each other. In the meantime, however, the important thing to remember is that other people have been through the same thing that you have—and they have survived. Many of them grew stronger from the experience, as they learned to take control of their finances in difficult times.

You can survive, too. Regardless of how you got into a financial crisis, it's never hopeless. Taking the practical steps outlined in this book can change the way you deal with money for the rest of your life. Some steps, like adjusting your income tax withholding, may seem so simple after you take them that you will wonder why you didn't take them sooner. One step at a time, you can make things better. You can take charge of your finances—and your life.

2   Quick Money Fixes

*Steps you can start taking —
while you read this book*

If you're having money troubles, the most important thing is that you take action now. You don't have any time to waste! The longer you wait, the worse your money situation will get. Stop all unnecessary expenditures until you have made a plan and you know what you can afford to spend. Here are some things you can do even before you read the whole book:

- Throw away catalogs and sale flyers without reading them.

- Stay away from the mall and the movies.

- Don't buy alcohol or cigarettes or go to bars.

- Don't eat out, especially at fast-food restaurants.

- Turn off the Home Shopping Network.

- Before you buy a new gadget or other item, ask yourself how you got along without it so far. If you got along fine, you can get along without it a while longer.

- Look at the food you have in your cupboards and refrigerator already, and only buy what you need to go with it. For example, if you already have cereal, you just need milk to go with it. Don't buy any more cereal until you've eaten what you have.

Help! I Can't Pay My Bills

- Take all shopping sites off your Favorites list on your computer. Don't go to eBay or any other shopping Web site just to see what's on sale.

- Take a sack lunch to work. A sandwich costs pennies to make.

- Take the bus or train to work. See if your employer subsidizes mass transit passes.

- Ride your bicycle to work if you can.

- Look at your credit card statements for recurring charges for items that you don't need. Cancel nonessential credit card insurance, online subscriptions, and other services.

- Raise the deductible (the amount you have to pay in an accident or other event) on your car and home insurance.

- If you have more than one car and can get by with only one, sell the extra car. Notify your insurance agency immediately so you can save on car insurance.

- Play with your kids. It's more fun for them to play with you than it is to get a new toy.

- If you always get a refund when you file your income tax return, file a new Form W-4 with your employer so you get more money every payday. Claim more withholding allowances to have less tax withheld from your pay.

- Cancel your cable TV package.

- Cancel your cell phone contract. If you are unemployed or have other extenuating circumstances, ask the cell phone company if you can cancel or suspend service without paying a cancellation fee.

- Go on a do-it-yourself binge. Cut your own hair, give yourself a pedicure, and wash your own car.

- If you don't have money for food, call a local food bank or religious organization. Charitable organizations often work together and can tell you where to find free food and possibly free hot meals.

Besides cutting expenses, see if you can earn some extra cash. Look around and see what services are in demand where you live that you can offer. Depending on your skills, you can offer babysitting, landscaping, tutoring, or housecleaning services. Or you may get after-hours work delivering pizza or stocking the shelves at the grocery store. When you are in a financial crisis, every dollar counts! For more suggestions, see chapter 9.

3 Find Out Where You Stand

Don't skip this chapter!

A struggling college student thinks that she can't budget her income and expenses because she doesn't have enough money. A businessman quits opening his bills when he doesn't have money to pay them. A dentist takes on more and more patients, refusing to examine his financial condition or his spending habits because he thinks he can earn his way out of debt. All three of these people are afraid to take a good, honest look at their finances. They think they can get out of trouble without ever finding out where they stand or making a plan any more specific than "make more money." Until they face the truth and put their financial situation on paper, however, their chances of success are very, very low.

"But I don't want to know how bad it is!" one of my friends says. "I just need to make more money. There's nothing to be gained by finding out how bad it is!"

There's nothing to be gained, that is, except the chance to make a realistic plan that can help you improve your situation—and a chance to finally be completely honest with yourself. The truth may be scary, but avoiding the truth is a lot scarier. Once you face up to reality, you should actually feel better, and certainly you'll feel more secure knowing that you are headed in the right direction.

No doubt, taking a good, honest look at your financial situation can be painful. If you've been avoiding it for a long time, it can be shocking. But it is absolutely essential. If you don't know how much money you have coming in and where it is going, how can you plan? If you don't know how much you owe, how can you decide what to pay first, or what else you can do to lower your debt? Not knowing where you stand financially is like driving up a mountain road with your eyes covered because you're afraid of the cliff on one side. It may be less scary to drive without looking, but it's going to hurt a lot worse when you drive over the edge!

Where you stand right now

It's time to take off the financial blindfold. First, let's look at what you own and what you owe. This will tell you where you stand financially at this point in time—or, in accountant talk, your "net worth."

Listing all your debts without also listing the things you own only shows you half of your financial picture. You need to see the whole picture to know where you really stand. The first thing you need to do is list the things you own that are—or can be converted into—cash.

You may be pleasantly surprised at what some things are worth. Your house may have increased in value, and a 401(k) plan you contributed to years ago may be worth more than you think. You may also find things you own that are dragging you down. That new car you bought may be going down in value faster than you can make the payments. You can make better choices once you know the facts.

Assignment 1:
Make a list of the things you own

Use the following Assets worksheet to list the things you own that are worth a significant amount of money. Don't be intimidated by the word "assets"—that's just accountant-speak for "things you own."

All the worksheets in this book can also be downloaded as Microsoft Office Excel documents at HelpICantPayMyBills.net. If you have a computer and access to the Internet, you may prefer the downloaded worksheets because they do the addition and subtraction automatically, are easy to change, and have additional features.

1. Gather information about your accounts at financial institutions. Find recent statements for:

   - Checking accounts

   - Savings accounts

   - Other financial institution accounts

   - Brokerage accounts

   - Retirement accounts

2. Add any other major valuables and their approximate value:

   - Home

   - Other real estate

   - Vehicles

   - Collector's items, precious metals

   - Amounts that other people or organizations owe to you, such as personal loans

You can estimate the value of noncash items by finding out what similar items sell for in the newspaper, at retail businesses, or at swap meets. The fastest way to find the approximate value of many items is on the Internet. Try looking at:

eBay. Go to http://www.ebay.com and look for recent sales of items similar to yours. Actual sales prices are more realistic than asking prices.

Online real estate valuations. Most realtors will gladly tell you the approximate value of your home. If you don't want to talk to a realtor and you want a quick answer, however, you can try an on-line service such as Zillow.com (http://www.zillow.com).

Kelley Blue Book. You can buy a paperback version of the standard Kelley Blue Book to help you determine the value of your vehicle, or you can go to http://www.kbb.com.

Don't worry for now about things you don't intend to sell, such as your leather couch, your fine china, or your career wardrobe. Stick to major items such as your home, bank account, and car.

	Assets	Date _____
	Asset (Bank or retirement account, real estate, vehicle)	**Balance or Market Value**
1		
2		
3		
4		
5		
6		
7		
8		
9		
10		
11		
12		
13		
14		
15		
16		
17		
18		
19		
20		
21		
22		
23		
24		
	Total	

Assignment 2: Make a list of your debts

Now for your debts. How much do you still owe on your car loan, your mortgage, and your student loans? What's the current balance on your credit and charge cards? Make a list of everything you owe (called "liabilities"), using the following Debts worksheet. If you don't have all the information, do the best you can. Include:

- Home mortgage
- Home equity line of credit
- Lines of credit
- Car loans
- Student loans
- Major credit cards
- Department store cards
- Personal loans you owe
- Overdue bills
- Taxes owed

Your Total Assets minus your Total Debts equals your Net Worth:

Total Assets   _____

Total Debts   –   _____

Net Worth   _____

In later chapters, I'll show you how to sort through your debts, get them reduced if possible, and start paying them off. By making a list of your debts, however, you've already taken a huge step toward becoming debt free. Give yourself credit!

	Creditor or Account Name	Balance	Interest Rate	Annual Fees	Minimum Monthly Payment	No. of Payments Left
	Debts					Date _____
1						
2						
3						
4						
5						
6						
7						
8						
9						
10						
11						
12						
13						
14						
15						
16						
17						
18						
19						
20						
21						
22						
23						
24						
Totals						

What are your income and expenses?

Looking at what you own and what you owe shows where you stand right now. A budget tells you where you're going and how to get there. To make real progress, you need both.

When young people first start getting a paycheck, they often see the next paycheck as the answer to all their problems. That next paycheck looks so big, so promising. Trouble is, by the time it gets here, it may have all been spent—or when they sit down to pay their bills, it doesn't go far. Oh well, the next paycheck will have to take care of the rest. By then, though, the mail has come several more times, and the table is piled high with bills.

The solution to the problem is knowing what your expenses are and planning ahead for next month—before the money is gone. That's all a budget is: a written list of expected income and expenses that helps you plan ahead better. Everyone needs one.

Some people seem to get along without a written budget, at least for a while. Either they make an awful lot of money to make up for any money management mistakes, or they are covering up their mistakes by adding more debt every year. To control their money and see where they're going, they need a written budget. Otherwise, they have a vague feeling that they're not managing their money very well, but they're not sure what to do. They may live from paycheck to paycheck, sometimes having to wait until payday to buy milk, and other times finding that after they pay the most urgent bills, there's nothing left. They think their spouses spend all the money—and their spouses think they do.

Although we all need a budget, most people dread making one. That's probably because they have the wrong idea about what a budget is and how it works.

Many people hate the word "budget." It reminds them too much of dieting—and they figure they will be able to stick with it about as long. They envision having to write down every 75-cent purchase, and they're afraid they won't be able to spend money on anything fun. Who wants that?

A good budget, however, doesn't stop you from spending any money or having any fun. It helps you make better choices with your money, which may allow you to have more fun! For example, you can look at your budget and decide that you'd rather spend $50 a month on books than on coffee, or that by spending a third less on clothes for a year, you can pay off your department store charge cards. The choices are yours. A budget keeps you from feeling guilty about spending every dollar at the same time that it puts *you*—not chance—in control of your priorities.

If you share your finances with someone, a budget can help bring harmony to your relationship. Without a budget, you might feel like the other person watches every purchase you make, waiting to pounce on every expenditure from kiwi fruit to new socks. Once you agree on a budget, however, you have a newfound freedom. You have a budget for food, and if you haven't gone over it (and you're not spending it all in the first week of the month), discussion ended. You have a clothing budget (you *do* have a clothing budget); it's OK to buy clothes that keep you warm, comfortable, and presentable. Far from restricting you, a budget forces both of you to come to an agreement on how you will spend your money—before you have a fight in the checkout line.

Making a current budget

The first steps to a budget are finding out what you're spending and estimating your income. This first budget will use what you make and spend now. In later chapters in this book, you will find ways to increase your income, reduce your expenses, or both.

Enter your monthly income on the Budget worksheet below, in the Current Monthly Amount column. If your income varies, use an average of the last few months. If your situation has changed—for instance, if you have been laid off—enter the amount you expect to receive under your current circumstances.

Look at your monthly bills for the last three months or so. Enter them on the Budget worksheet, using the approximate amount you spend in each expense category. Don't worry about the Goal Monthly Amount and the Difference columns for now; just fill in the Current Monthly Amount.

Once you've reconstructed your monthly bills, add up your daily and miscellaneous expenses and continue to fill in approximate amounts for each category. How much do you spend on newspapers, or on food from vending machines and the company cafeteria? Using canceled checks, credit card statements, pay stubs, and receipts, re-create your patterns. If it looks like you should have a lot more left over every month than you really do, look closer. Have you forgotten

Help! I Can't Pay My Bills

Budget

Date _____

Income	Current Monthly Amount	Goal Monthly Amount	Difference
Income (enter gross pay before taxes and withholding)			

Expense Category			
FIXED EXPENSES - Expenses that generally stay the same			
1 Cable and Internet service			
2 Car insurance			
3 Car payments			
4 Child care			
5 Credit card payments			
6 Health insurance			
7 Homeowner's or renter's insurance			
8 Income tax withheld from earnings			
9 Membership fees			
10 Other debt payments			
11 Other insurance			
12 Payroll taxes and other deductions from earnings			
13 Rent or mortgage payment			
14 Tuition, education expenses			
15 Other fixed expenses			
VARIABLE EXPENSES - Expenses that vary from month to month			
16 Car maintenance			
17 Clothing			
18 Dining Out			
19 Gas and oil (for car)			
20 Gifts			
21 Groceries			
22 Household repairs and maintenance			
23 Medical expenses not covered by insurance			
24 Miscellaneous			
25 Other transportation expenses (bus fare, taxi fare)			
26 Pet care			
27 Telephone bill			
28 Utilities			
29 Vacations, trips			
TOTAL EXPENSES			
INCOME MINUS EXPENSES			

ATM withdrawals? Or did you not count items that were "just that once"? There will always be one-time expenses, so be sure to allow for them.

If you pay any bills less than once a month, such as tuition, property taxes, or insurance premiums, calculate how much they actually cost you per month and enter them on the form. For example, if you pay $600 in car insurance every six months, fill in $100 ($600 divided by 6) as your monthly car insurance expense.

Add up your expenses. This should be about how much you are spending right now. If it seems low, make sure you haven't forgotten something. It is very important that you find all your expenses: Forgetting an expense category is one of the most common reasons budgets fail.

Subtract your expenses from your income. If the result is a small number, or even a negative number, don't panic! The main thing here is to find your starting point. As you read the rest of the book, you will find ways to change things for the better, and you'll go through the process of balancing your budget and making it work.

That's it! Making a current budget is a lot of work. Many people never make a budget in their lives; by making one, you have taken a giant step toward a better future.

What if your income is unpredictable?

Budgeting is definitely a challenge if you are self-employed or if you are paid sporadically. How can you figure out how much you can spend if you never know when you'll get paid? Unfortunately, the people who find it hardest to budget also need it the most. Without a budget, you don't know exactly what your minimum expenses are, let alone what it takes to live comfortably. You can easily fall into the trap of thinking that when the next big check comes, everything will be fine. Unfortunately, the next big check is too often spoken for before it comes. It is better to look squarely at your monthly expenses than to keep trying frantically to cover your bills as money comes in.

Sometimes making a budget forces people to face the fact that what they are doing to make a living isn't working. Maybe it never will, or maybe it needs to be supplemented with something else until it does. It's better to know than to keep wondering why you just can't seem to make it, month after month.

Now what?

When you have completed the worksheets in this chapter, you should know what you own, what you owe, and how much money it takes to keep you going every month. For some people, this might be the first time in their lives that they have put this all down on paper and added it up—no easy task in the best of circumstances! Even—or especially—if the numbers look discouraging, don't stop now. Keep the momentum going. We're going to put your hard work to good use!

Keep these worksheets handy. You will refer to them as you work through the rest of this book.

4

What Not to Do in a Financial Crisis

Denial, desperate risk taking,
and giving up only make
things worse

It's tempting to want to find an easy way out of financial distress, but the "easy" way never is. Living in denial about your financial state may seem easier in the short term, but it doesn't solve anything. Taking big risks in hope of a windfall, such as making investments based on hot tips or gambling outright, can make things much, much worse. Just plain giving up is not the answer, either. Even if you go through foreclosure and bankruptcy, your struggles are not over.

When people are in a money pinch, they can easily fall prey to all kinds of schemes and pitfalls. Many profiteers pretend that they want to help, when in reality they are like hyenas, circling around individuals at their most vulnerable times. Becoming aware of the traps that many people fall into can help you avoid them.

Denial and avoidance

The first trap to avoid is denial. Yes, it hurts to face the truth. It's worse than getting weighed at the doctor's office. You don't weigh any more after the nurse writes the number down, though, and you aren't any poorer when you stop denying and avoiding your finances.

Some of us have gone to great lengths to avoid money-related pain. Sometimes our avoidance efforts are almost funny. Other times they are just counterproductive. For example:

- **Not opening mail.** Contrary to what it feels like sometimes, not everything that comes in the mail is a bill. It could be a survey, a coupon you can use, or maybe even a rebate check. If it *is* a bill, you need to at least open it and make sure it's right, before it's too late to protest it.

- **Not organizing a stack of bills before starting to pay them.** I helped someone who was in terrible financial straits organize his bills, so we could determine what he should pay first. His strategy had been that whenever he got a little money, he would start paying bills from the top of the stack until the money was gone. I discovered that many bills had been paid twice and actually had a credit balance. Other bills went unpaid, even though some were small enough that he could easily have paid them and gotten the collection agencies off his case. What got paid and what didn't was totally random.

- **Being afraid to answer the phone.** It doesn't take very many calls from collection agencies to make a person start to tense up when the phone rings. It's tempting to stop answering it altogether. It's one thing to let the phone ring when a particularly nasty collector takes on your case and calls every day, especially if the collector is in the wrong, but not answering the phone on a regular basis is a sign of avoidance.

By reading this book, you are taking positive action—the opposite of denial. Once you start to follow the steps in this book and improve your financial situation, you won't want to hide from the truth anymore.

Bankruptcy

Bankruptcy is seldom a good solution. The winners in bankruptcy are the bankruptcy professionals, lawyers, and trustees, who get to take their fees off the top. The losers are usually everybody else.

Many writers have bemoaned the new bankruptcy laws and how they make it harder for people. The truth is, bankruptcy was never such a hot deal in the first place. If you're looking for a way to throw up your hands and give up, bankruptcy isn't the answer—and it never was. You think you have too much paperwork to deal with now? You haven't seen anything until you have to deal with all the paperwork of a bankruptcy. You want your creditors to go away? They will, for now—but they won't be lining up to lend you money afterward, either, after bankruptcy practically kills your credit score. You're embarrassed and tired of the shame of being behind in your bills? Bankruptcy is a public procedure. You'll have to appear in court and deal with your creditors, sometimes face-to-face. Bankruptcy notices appear in the local paper.

Bankruptcy is filed as of a certain date. It can take months or years for the bankruptcy to be settled, and by that time, you may be deep in debt again. Of course, bankruptcy can't help with any new bills that come after the bankruptcy date.

Most of the bills that can be discharged in bankruptcy could be negotiated or dealt with without filing for bankruptcy. Credit card companies, for example, would much rather negotiate with you than have you file for bankruptcy because they are likely to receive more that way. Hospitals will generally work with you to create a payment plan.

On the other hand, bankruptcy generally won't get you out of back taxes or your mortgage. It won't erase past or future child support payments. You can't generally use bankruptcy to get rid of student loans.

What is a Chapter 7 bankruptcy?

Chapter 7 is a court-supervised procedure that takes what you own, sells it or otherwise converts it to cash, and pays your creditors. Depending on your state's laws, you may be able to keep all or most of your property, including your house and car. The courts use your money and the cash from the sale of your things to pay debts in a certain order, according to state law. You then receive a discharge, which means that certain debts are gone and you no longer owe them.

What is a Chapter 13 bankruptcy?

Generally, a Chapter 13 is not what people think of as bankruptcy at all, because it does not immediately erase your debts. Instead, you make a plan to repay your creditors over a three- to five-year period. If the court approves your plan, you are then protected from lawsuits, garnishments, and other creditor action while the plan is in effect. The trustee may charge about 10% of the amount of the plan as a fee, and you should hire an attorney, who will have to be paid.

How do the new bankruptcy laws affect me?

The new bankruptcy laws make it harder to get a Chapter 7 bankruptcy and thus simply get rid of debts. If you have a good source of income, you will probably have to file for Chapter 13 bankruptcy instead and create a plan to pay your bills. Whether you file for Chapter 7 or Chapter 13 bankruptcy, you also must go to financial counseling.

What you do get rid of when you file for bankruptcy is a lot of control over your finances. Before you file for bankruptcy, you have some measure of financial privacy, and you decide where your money goes. Once you file, whether for Chapter 7 or Chapter 13, you have very little to say. Everything you own must be accounted for, and some assets may be sold. While a creditor might have been happy to accept small monthly payments, under a Chapter 7 bankruptcy, everything you own that does not qualify for an exclusion must be liquidated to pay as much as possible of the total balance you owe.

Bankruptcy doesn't solve most financial problems

The real problem with most bankruptcies is that they don't solve underlying problems. Many people defend the rights of individuals to have their debts erased with Chapter 7 bankruptcies, arguing that "you can't expect them to live on what they get paid." Well, if they couldn't live on that before, they won't be able to afterward, either—especially if the only credit they qualify for after the bankruptcy carries high fees and interest rates. Clearly, a repetitive cycle of ringing up debts and having them discharged through bankruptcy is not the answer to low wages and a high cost of living. Any lasting solution must include a better financial plan with lower expenses, higher income, or both.

Bankruptcy hurts innocent people

To hear many people talk, debt collection is a struggle between the cold, heartless credit card companies and poor individuals. They see bankruptcy as an act of mercy or as a way of evening the score. What harm is there in erasing an unfortunate person's debts and giving her a fresh start?

However, to the extent that people have actually made purchases or used services, turning around and filing for bankruptcy has exactly the same effect as shoplifting. The other customers have to foot the bill. I read an article that said it's OK to go bankrupt, because you've been paying the cost of other people's bankruptcies all these years yourself in higher prices and interest rates. Under that rationale, shoplifting is fine, too—but we all know that it isn't. If someone racks up a bill when he has a heart attack and spends a week in the ICU, he doesn't have a choice (except perhaps to be better insured). However, when people routinely spend more than they make and then expect to have their debts cleared off, somebody else is paying the bills they don't.

"But it's a big corporation," people say. Big corporations are owned by small individuals like you and me. Their shareholders are more likely to be retired people on fixed incomes who own a few of the corporation's shares than corporate fat cats. When everyone thinks that big corporations can take it, the customers and shareholders have to pay. Nothing comes for free.

If you can't feel sorry for credit companies, think about the small businesses and individuals who are on the receiving end of bankruptcies. When you file for bankruptcy, you give up the right to determine who gets paid. The small contractor, your landlord, and any private individuals you have borrowed from will suffer. Have you ever played with dominoes, setting them up in a row so all you have to do is touch one and the rest all fall down? That's how bankruptcy works: People go bankrupt and force other people into financial hardship or bankruptcy, and on it goes. If someone has cosigned with you, she still has to pay the whole bill. Many people promise that they will pay individuals after they go bankrupt, but they seldom actually do.

Sometimes people are determined to file for bankruptcy. I knew a physician named Chad who got behind in his bills and was sure bankruptcy would solve his problems. He went to a respectable lawyer, who told him that he had too many assets to qualify for bankruptcy and that he was better off just paying his bills, even if he had to sell something. Unfortunately, Chad didn't like that answer, and he shopped around until he found a paralegal who was more than happy to help him file for bankruptcy. The first thing the paralegal told him to do was to stop paying his bills and instead send him $2,000. You would have thought that sounded suspicious enough, but Chad did as he was told. Of course, by not paying his bills and sending his money elsewhere, Chad soon more than qualified to file for bankruptcy. The paralegal advertised a low bankruptcy fee, but that was just the beginning.

By the time Chad paid all the fees and expenses, filing for bankruptcy turned out to be extremely expensive, and he was much worse off than before. He could have made arrangements with creditors, sold some things, and worked it out. Instead, he gave control of everything he owned to the bankruptcy court. He spent over $5,000 on legal and bankruptcy fees, lost everything, and never recovered financially—and it was totally unnecessary.

When is filing for bankruptcy a good idea?

Sometimes, bankruptcy may be the best remaining option. It may be a good idea as a last resort in situations like these, for example:

- Your debts are the result of a one-time disaster, such as a failed business, catastrophic medical expenses, or someone else going bankrupt and owing you a large sum of money.

- You are liable for insurmountable debts that belonged to someone else, such as an ex-spouse.

Foreclosure

Anyone who has struggled to keep up mortgage payments when times get tough can understand the desire to "just give it back to the bank." When you're tired of struggling, foreclosure seems like one way to simply give up. Also, unlike filing for bankruptcy, you don't have to do anything to be foreclosed on: You stop making payments, and the bank does the rest.

While letting your home go into foreclosure may seem like the easy way out, it isn't. Think about the consequences:

- **You lose your home.** You have to live somewhere, and moving and getting into another place won't be cheap.

- **You lose all your equity.** Think about your down payment, the principal you paid off bit by bit with your mortgage payments, and the time and money you spent painting and fixing up the place. With foreclosure, that's all gone.

- **You might still owe money!** If the lender gets less money from the property than you owe, you may be sued (in some states) for the difference. If the lender takes a loss, *you* may have to pay tax on the amount of the loss—even though you never see any money.

- **Your credit score tanks.** Losing your house to foreclosure is one of the worst things you can do to your credit history. A foreclosure on your record can haunt you when you apply for credit, try to rent an apartment, or even apply for a job, for years to come.

Hot Tips

Watch out for Hot Tips. Hot Tips are usually given either by friends of friends or by excited-sounding salespeople. These tips may show up at work, on your TV screen, or in your e-mail in-box. Ignore them. They'll get you all excited, take money you can't afford to lose, and leave you depressed and more broke than before.

Kathy called me all excited about a new investment opportunity that her daughter had heard about at work. The scoop is that the Iraqi dollar is available for sale, as of the next day. If you buy it now, you can buy many Iraqi dollars with each U.S. dollar. When the Iraqi economy improves, so the story goes, the Iraqi dollars should be worth the same as U.S. dollars, and you can be a millionaire in a matter of months! Kathy "knew" this was real because some of her other friends had also heard about it.

I hated to spoil the fun, but this Hot Tip has a few flaws:

- Iraq uses dinars, not dollars, so I wonder about anyone who refers to Iraqi money as dollars.

- There is no force that naturally brings one currency, such as dinars, into a 1:1 value ratio with another currency. That's not how it works.

- Kathy said that you are supposed to invest on a daily basis and sell before the markets close every day. To invest in any long-term recovery of the Iraq economy, you would need to stay invested considerably longer than one day.

This Hot Tip came by word of mouth and through the Internet. Neither the *Wall Street Journal* nor *Barron's* said a word about it. (No, the financial journalists didn't conspire to keep it out of the news so they could make all the money.)

Fortunately, Kathy is too smart to part with her money until she gets some good advice. After a stockbroker told her that she'd have better luck with turkey futures ("gobble, gobble," in his words), she dropped the idea. Unfortunately, many people rush to act on Hot Tips, only to lose again and again.

What makes a Hot Tip really take off? Usually it contains a so-called secret—something people feel lucky, even special, to have found out. There's often a deadline: Better hurry, this one might get away! Often a Hot Tip slams other tips as frauds, to prove to you that they are different from the rest. If they throw in a conspiracy theory and send it to a few hundred of their closest e-mail buddies, they may have an Internet hit!

Not all tips are as easy to see through as the Iraqi dinar story. You can get a Hot Tip about a respectable company's stock, and the tip may even have some truth to it. Be wary of following any investment advice that you don't fully understand. If you've never taken

Books on Buying Stocks

If you want to buy individual stocks, I recommend reading these books first:

One Up on Wall Street: How To Use What You Already Know to Make Money in the Market, by Peter Lynch

How to Make Money in Stocks: A Winning System in Good Times or Bad, by William J. O'Neil, founder of *Investor's Business Daily*

economics and don't understand the currency markets, stay out of currency trading. Don't buy individual stocks until you study the stock market and understand the basics, and make sure you are willing to stay informed as long as you own stocks. Unless you're a professional, don't touch stock options and futures. Never send money to people who send you e-mail or snail mail pitches— *especially* if they breathlessly tell you how very rich you will soon be. You can't afford to lose money to these Hot Tips, but even more important, you can't afford to be demoralized when you realize you've been had.

Over-hyped business ideas

I love small business. Small businesses are exciting, and the right small business can lead to a satisfying career and financial success. Small businesses can even lead to wealth; most millionaires made their money that way.

However, some businesses cost too much, are too risky, or promise more than they will ever deliver. Some are outright scams. Here are some types of businesses you should generally avoid:

What is a Franchise?

Franchises are businesses like Subway or Dairy Queen, where you buy the right to open a business with the franchise name. You use the company's distribution system, follow its rules, and benefit from its reputation and advertising.

- **Businesses that require a substantial investment that you can't afford to lose.** No business is a sure thing, and most will require more money to keep them going in the beginning than one would hope. Even the best business can go under if you don't have enough money to keep it afloat long enough.

- **Heavily advertised businesses that seem to promote how much money you will make, with hardly any effort or inconvenience.** Little is said about the service or business you will provide or how you will benefit your customers. You see pictures of couples boarding their own Learjets, and you're asked to envision what your life will be like with unlimited money. Real businesses are about pleasing customers and having savvy management skills. These businesses require long hours and a lot of effort.

- **Businesses that "anyone" can do.** If anyone can do it, why should you be interested? How are you going to excel at something anyone can do? Find something that uses your extraordinary gifts, and do something that everyone else is *not* doing.

- **Many multilevel marketing (MLM) businesses.** Some people definitely make money in MLMs, but many people spend more on product and promotional materials than they make. If people try to sell to family and friends, which many MLMs want them to do, they may lose a few friends in the process.

The right MLM, joined for the right reasons and with realistic expectations, can be a good small business. Before you join an MLM, ask yourself:

1. Is the emphasis of this MLM on a great product or service, or on how much money everyone will make? Successful businesses have an exceptional product or service to sell.

2. Would you buy this product or service otherwise? Would people rather buy this from an individual such as yourself or pick it up at the mall or the grocery store?

3. Does the MLM require me to invest time or money that I can't afford to lose right now?

4. Is the primary market my friends and relatives? (You only have so many of them.)

5. Will I spend most of my profits on buying more product for myself?

Think of it this way: If selling this product or service would be a good idea even if it weren't an MLM, then you may be able to make a go of it. Otherwise, save your time and energy.

- **Overpriced franchises.** Some franchises are great opportunities and are well worth the investment, especially those with a well-known name. Other franchises are mostly hot air. Consider what you are actually buying with your franchise. If most of the money is supposedly for training and support, and the franchise name is not well known, watch out. If the company promises that it will help you find clients and customers, think about what your recourse will be when it doesn't work out, or when the home office stops returning your calls.

- **Any business opportunity that does not take into account your skills and experience.** It can be a good business, but not right for you—at least not yet.

Paying too much for investing "secrets"

Investing seminars and newsletters are a huge business. People pay thousands of dollars for them. However, they often find that a good share of the time or print is spent trying to convince them that what they really need is the next seminar or newsletter—which just happens to cost even more. Many people spent $20,000 going to seminars from a very popular national investment guru. Too bad that guru's own investments have done so poorly that he's filed for bankruptcy!

Sometimes there's a fine line between legitimate advice and overpriced hype. In the '90s, I read an investing book that impressed me so much that I signed up for the author's newsletter. It was mostly well written and offered good advice, but a large portion of the newsletter was spent trying to sell us the author's other specialized newsletter that would tell us what we really needed to know—and another, and another. We always seemed to be one newsletter short of knowing the ultimate investing secrets. I figured one newsletter was enough (it wasn't cheap!), and I followed his advice, selling most of my stock investments when he said that all the signs pointed to a drop-off. However, stocks didn't go down, they went up. He had told us to sell right before one of the greatest stock price increases in history! Nobody's perfect, so I could forgive him for that—until his newsletter showed the stock market increases and claimed that he had told everyone to buy, not sell, at the very beginning of the steep incline. I found my old newsletters: Sure enough, he had changed his advice after the fact! I canceled my subscription.

Steer clear of anyone who tries to sell you *amazing secrets*. There are no secrets to good, sound investing. You can learn everything you need from books and magazines you can get from the library for free. For current investment news, I'm partial to the *Wall Street Journal*. I read the online version every morning. It doesn't get the heart racing quite like a good pitch for another investment seminar, but it keeps me informed. *Investor's Business Daily* also has excellent information for investors. Pick up a copy of the *Wall Street Journal* or *Investor's Business Daily* at the newsstand, read it at the library, or subscribe online (for a fee) at http://www.wsj.com or http://www.investors.com.

Gambling

The more desperate people are financially, the more susceptible they are to the lure of gambling. Gambling used to be socially unacceptable in many circles, but now that state governments use lotteries to raise money for worthy causes like education, gambling has lost most of its stigma. Gambling didn't get a bad name in the first place for no reason, however, and as gambling becomes more popular, we may be forced to remember what those reasons were.

The chances of anyone winning in gambling over the long term are so slim as to be nonexistent. You might as well stand by the side of the road and hope somebody accidentally drops a bag of money out of her car.

The worst thing that can happen to you is that you win when you start gambling. I have a friend who used to eat lunch with his coworkers at a casino. The food was good, and they would laugh at the fools sticking their money in the slot machines. Then one day he tried his luck with just a few dollars. He won over $5,000. From that time on, he was hooked. He lost that $5,000 many times over, and then he tried to chase that money with more. He was ashamed of his problem, and he started avoiding his friends. His marriage was strained, and he was evicted from his apartment—twice. This friend is exceptionally smart and hardworking, but gambling has cost him more than he will be able to recover for a long time.

To hear people talk on Monday morning, most gamblers win, or at least break even, on their weekend in Vegas or at the local casino. They must have selective memories, however. If you ever doubt it, look at the gaudy buildings in Vegas. They didn't build those casinos by giving money away!

If you want to indulge in recreational gambling, do it only when your bills are paid and you can afford it, and stay fully aware that gambling is entertainment, not an investment strategy. People in financial distress are much too vulnerable to the get-rich-quick dream, however. The best thing they can do is to find some other form of entertainment—and almost any other way to get out of financial trouble.

Step Two

Come Up with Some with Some Cash

5 Sell Something!

*Get quick cash by
selling extra stuff*

When you're having trouble paying your bills, even a small amount of cash can help you get by. One thing you can do is look around and see what you can convert to cash. Your financial situation determines how much you need to sell—whether you need to turn some miscellaneous knickknacks into cash for groceries or sell larger items so you can catch up on your bills. If you are way behind in your bills and mortgage payments, you may need to sell your car or even your house.

It's easier than ever to turn your books, clothing, household items, and even cars into much-needed cash. Most of us have things that we don't use or could live without. Some stuff even costs us money the longer we keep it. Owners of mini storage businesses know that people often pay $100 or more per month to store stuff that they never come back to retrieve. You can pay a lot for insurance and maintenance on cars, boats, and motorcycles whether you use them or not; plus, the older they get, the less they are usually worth.

Even if you only have outgrown children's clothes and an exercise machine nobody uses, you might be able to get something from them. If you look around, you might find an extra $500 to $3,000 from things you have right now.

What can you sell?

The easiest things to sell are the things that many people need, or want, and it helps if they can easily tell exactly what they are getting. For example, a popular book in near-new condition is a cinch to re-sell. So are necessities like major appliances. I recently advertised some furniture and other household items for sale, and the first evening the phone rang nonstop. Unfortunately, they all wanted the washer and dryer; I'm still stuck with the rest. Practical items that are not dependent on style and color sell quickly.

When you're looking for things to sell, first think about things you don't use anymore. If you have kids, you probably have out-grown clothes and toys you can sell. Kids now start riding bicycles so young that they can go through several sizes, and the outgrown ones are always in demand. If you don't use your exercise equip-ment, there's no point in keeping it. It's just an expensive laundry rack that makes you feel guilty every time you look at it. Sell it—and find some exercise you don't hate! That home gym might be just the thing for someone else.

Next, look for things you can do without that are costing you money. If you have a vacation home or a time-share, it may have to go. The same goes for investment property, especially if it costs you money every month. Most families can get by with one car if they have to, and if you live near public transportation you may be able to get by with no car. You may need the occasional taxi ride, but a taxi fare now and then is nothing compared to the monthly cost of own-ing a car.

Animals can be almost as expensive to maintain as children. If selling your dog or cat sounds like selling one of your kids, hope-fully you can find a way to avoid such a drastic measure. I know how tough it is: When I couldn't pay my bills twenty-some years ago, I had to give my beautiful red Doberman back to her original owners. I could buy food for my baby, or I could buy 50-pound bags of dog food. The baby won. Horses are even more expensive to keep than dogs and cats. Deciding whether you can afford to keep an animal can be one of the hardest decisions you have to make. If you can't keep a pet, try to sell it rather than give it away. Not only is some cash better than none, but putting up cash shows commitment from the new owners and hopefully means that they can provide for your pet.

Don't overlook selling things that you can make or grow. If you have an orchard or a blueberry patch, you may be able to sell your produce at a roadside stand or a farmer's market. If you make garden benches or crafts items, you may find a market for them at holiday bazaars and such. Be sure to add up your expenses. Start small, and make sure that you can sell things at a reasonable profit before you invest too much time and money. You will usually get the best prices if your product is different or original. For more ideas, see "Your Own Business" in chapter 9.

In difficult financial times, you may have to part with just about anything you can sell to get by. You'll find that you can live without a stereo system, or even a TV. (One consolation when you sell electronics is that by the time your financial situation improves, the new models will have come out—inevitably better and at lower prices.) If you have collectibles and antiques, you might have to sell some to raise cash. You may even need to sell your home. There is a certain freedom in discovering what you can do without. Remember, virtually nothing but family and friends is irreplaceable.

Should you sell your house?

Unless you are taking a job elsewhere, it's rarely a good idea to sell your house to pay your bills. For one thing, your house is probably your best investment. When people reach retirement age, often their most valuable asset is a home that's paid for. Unless you are still relatively young, selling your home to pay your bills may keep you from ever realizing that goal. It can be difficult to get into another home, especially if you are in financial trouble, and if you wait to buy again, home prices can skyrocket out of your range in the meantime.

Another problem is that selling costs can easily be 10% to 15% of what your home sells for, so you may not get as much cash out of your house as you had hoped. If you bought a bigger house than you can now afford and you want to sell it and buy a smaller one, the new house will have to be quite a bit less expensive to make up for the expense of selling one home and buying another. Otherwise, you could end up with less house but no more money and just as big a mortgage as when you started.

If you are not behind in your mortgage payments but you think you may be forced into bankruptcy, think twice before selling your home. The laws vary by state, but generally your home is exempt from having to be sold to pay creditors in a bankruptcy. If you sell your home, most of the cash you get from the sale may be used to pay creditors.

If you are behind in your mortgage payments and the bank is threatening to foreclose on your house and take it away from you, you need to either find a way to catch up on your payments or sell your home. Foreclosure is one of the worst things that can happen to your finances and your credit history; do whatever you can to avoid it.

Beware the foreclosure vultures! Once the bank puts out a public notice that it has initiated foreclosure proceedings, they start circling. These are people who make a business of finding out what houses are being foreclosed on and how much the owners owe on them (all a matter of public record). They try to buy the property for not much more than the amount owed. Some homeowners report receiving as many as sixty-five calls and letters in one week from people offering to "help" them avoid foreclosure. As a rule, they are not in the business of paying a fair price for houses—they're looking for steals. It's better if you sell your house some other way. If you haven't waited too long, you may still be able to sell your home to a legitimate buyer at a price that doesn't rob you of all your equity.

Six ways to sell things

The best way to sell any given thing depends on:

- Who the likely buyers are

- Where people look for the things you want to sell

- Your skills and the resources available to you

- How quickly you need the money

First, put yourself in the position of your potential buyers. Where do the people who want this type of thing live? Are you selling strollers, camping gear, and other things that appeal to families? Are you selling specialized things like antique silverware that someone who lives thousands of miles away may be looking for? Think about how you would go about looking if you wanted to buy them. Would you look in the classified ads, or would you pull over at a garage sale to look for these things?

Be sure you are reaching people who not only want what you're selling but can afford to buy it. I advertised a used tractor unsuccessfully in the local paper several times. I set it in the front yard during a neighborhood garage sale, and the tractor attracted many admirers but no buyers. I live near lots of small farms, so I didn't think a tractor would be that hard to sell! I soon decided that the problem wasn't finding people who wanted a tractor, it was finding people who could afford to buy one—at least without store financing. I figured that the people I worked with were more likely to be able to afford a tractor, so I placed a free ad in my workplace newsletter. Sure enough, a man drove up pulling a flatbed trailer (that seemed like a good sign) and bought the tractor. Once I found the right market, the tractor was as good as sold.

Depending on how quickly you need to raise money, you may want to start with the least expensive way of selling something, and try something else if that doesn't work.

Word of mouth

The cheapest way to sell something is by word of mouth. You'd be surprised what you can sell just by letting people know that it's available. I sold a house to a friend of a friend—fortunately before I listed the house with an agent. The buyer got a good deal on a house in the country, and I saved over $10,000 in real estate commissions. Selling this way doesn't always work, but if you have time, it's worth a try.

People are sometimes more interested in something that they hear about by word of mouth. Perhaps they hope to get a good deal before everybody else hears about it, or maybe they trust the person selling it. If they know someone who is selling a decent car, they'd rather buy that than a car from a stranger who may be unloading a lemon.

Some people, especially relatives, may even buy things as a way to help out or to keep things in the family. I once paid a fair price for some collectibles from a relative who was selling them to raise cash. He was happy to see the collectibles stay in the family, and I see them as a long-term investment. Besides, they're cool.

If you have something to sell, start by telling your friends and family. You might be afraid to put them on the spot by asking them if they want to buy something, but you can always ask them if they know someone who may be interested. You never know who might want something, or know someone who does.

Garage sales

If you need money by this weekend, how about a garage sale? You don't need large items to sell; you can make a pretty good cash haul by selling lots of little things. In fact, small items often go the fastest at garage sales.

To get people to stop and get out of their cars, you need to have an impressive pile of stuff set out where people can see it. If you don't have a traffic-stopping display, try combining your efforts with another family's. Then you can put the magic words "Multi-Family Garage Sale" on your signs and get more interest.

You might also want to have a joint garage sale if you live on a street that doesn't get much traffic, or if there's no place to set up or for shoppers to park. If you have a friend who lives in a better garage sale location, you can offer to do more of the work in exchange for using her place.

One hazard of joint garage sales, however, is how interesting the other seller's stuff often looks. If you're not careful, you will be each other's best customers. It's a bad sign if you go home with more stuff than you came with!

Bulletin boards

The great thing about bulletin boards is that they are usually free. A bulletin board in the right place can be very effective. If you are trying to sell a house near your workplace, for example, the bulletin board in the coffee-break room may be just the place to find prospective buyers. Grocery stores, coffee shops, and libraries also sometimes have bulletin boards where you can post flyers or index cards. Be sure to follow the bulletin board owners' rules, and get permission if necessary. Otherwise, your ad may land in the trash before anyone sees it.

Classified ads

Classified ads usually don't cost too much to run, especially in smaller papers. They are a good way to sell things that are difficult or impossible to ship, or things that people want to see in person before they buy. You can usually place an ad and have it come out within a few days—an important consideration if you need cash quickly.

People look for certain items in classified ads more than others. Many people buy cars through them; at least half of the classified ads in many papers are for vehicles. Pets sell well in classified ads because people want to pick out and buy pets locally. Most papers also have sections for musical instruments, sporting goods, and other common items.

You can even run a classified ad to advertise your garage sale. If you have some items that will sell easily, such as appliances or tools, include them in the ad. People may come to check out your easy-to-sell items and, while they're at it, find other goodies that they can't live without.

It's harder to sell real estate through the classifieds. It's hard to tell much about a house and its neighborhood from a small ad, and buyers can look online for houses and get all kinds of information and pictures. That doesn't mean you shouldn't try to sell a house with a classified ad, but if you are in any hurry, you may want buyers to be able to find your house other ways, too.

Furniture and other household items are tricky to sell in classified ads. Few people want to bother calling, setting up an appointment, and driving out to see a small item. They might spend an hour going to see a couch—only to discover that they don't like it. You can make it easier for them by including a digital picture (if the classified ad provides such a service) or a link to a picture on a picture-sharing Web site.

eBay, Amazon, and other sales Web sites

The more people who can find the thing you want to sell, the better your chance of selling it and getting a good price. When you list items online, millions of people can find them. Admittedly, other millions of people are also trying to sell things online, so you've got some stiff competition. Still, if you have something to sell that is in demand, you're almost sure to find a willing buyer online.

Some people hesitate to sell things online because they aren't sure how it works. A common misconception is that you may have to sell things for practically nothing if you don't get many bidders. You'd be afraid to list an expensive clock if someone might pick it up on a slow day for $5. Don't worry: Just set the minimum price you're willing to take, and if nobody bids at least that much, it won't sell. On many sites, you don't even have to use bidding to sell things; you can simply set a price and wait for a buyer.

One reason that people have become comfortable buying on eBay and other online services is that they can see how many sales any given seller has made and what percentage of the seller's customers gave positive feedback. This is great when you are a buyer, but it can put you at a disadvantage if you are new at online selling and you just want to sell a few things. You have no track record, and everyone can see that. One way around this problem is to have someone who has built up a track record online list things for you. Maybe you have a friend who is a veteran online seller. You can also find people who make a living listing items online for others. They take a percentage of the sale amount, but their help can easily pay for itself if it gets you a better price for your items. They generally take digital pictures for you (an essential online sales tool), keep your items until they sell, and ship the sold goods to customers.

Books are some of the easiest things to sell online, especially books that look new or almost new. Amazon.com and Half.com let you list books on their Web sites, alongside their new books. You must follow their pricing guidelines, and you must accurately describe the condition of the book according to their standards. The buyer pays all or most (usually all) of the shipping cost. Some books sell very quickly: I once resold a popular diet book in less than an hour, after deciding that I would starve to death on the eating plan it recommended. Other books depend a bit more on luck: There may be someone out there who really wants your Windows 98 book. Or maybe not.

Don't overlook specialty Web sites. You can find sites that specialize in anything from quilting to *Star Trek* figurines. I have LEGOs in their original boxes from my ninth birthday—back when LEGOs was really a building toy. My sets with windows, doors, and shingles are much more versatile and way cooler than the models they sell today. I just discovered a site where people buy and sell sets like mine. Because the site attracts people specifically interested in LEGOs, the sets sell for decent prices.

Real estate agents

If you're not in a big hurry and you're willing to do some work, it's possible to sell a house yourself. You don't need a real estate company to fill out paperwork; you can pay an escrow company to do that for you, at a fraction of what a real estate agent charges. Most of the money you pay a real estate agent is for finding a buyer, and if you can do that yourself, you can save thousands of dollars.

If you need to sell your home fast—for example, if you are moving or if you are in danger of losing your home to foreclosure—you may need an agent. Agents can usually sell your home more quickly because they work with buyers every day. They can also put your house on the all-important Multiple Listing Service (MLS), the list that other agents and their clients use to find property. In fact, it's very likely that when you bought your house an agent helped you find it in the MLS. People can still find a house by driving down the street and seeing a sign, but they are more likely to find your house if it is listed by a real estate agent and included in the MLS. The more people who see what you have for sale, the more demand there will be for it, and the more you should be able to get for it.

Another advantage of using a real estate agent is that you avoid the awkwardness of dealing with sellers. You don't have to let strangers into your house to show it to them, and when the house sells, all the paperwork is taken care of. If the complexity of selling a house makes you nervous, paying an agent may be worth it for your peace of mind.

What not to sell

Selling things can be exciting—even addicting. Getting a phone call or an online order can be the best news you've heard all day. In your

Do Your Homework

If you are interested in selling your own home, I recommend reading *The For Sale by Owner Handbook: FSBO FAQS: From Pricing Your Home Right and Increasing Its Curb Appeal to Negotiating the Contract and Hassle-free Closing*, by Piper Nichole.

enthusiasm, don't get carried away and sell things you shouldn't or sell things too cheaply. For example, unless you are moving, it's rarely a good idea to sell your essential furniture and appliances, because you will have a hard time replacing them for the price you received.

Don't let people pressure you into selling them things that you don't want to part with. It's not unusual for people to come to see one item and then spot something else that they like. Especially if they think you are desperate, they may try to buy something for next to nothing, or to talk you into selling something that's irreplaceable or that you don't realize the value of. Don't fall for it. Get a second opinion, or check online to see what similar items are selling for. When in doubt, wait.

6 Get Back What People Owe You

Many people could pay their bills if they only had the money that other people owe them. Unfortunately, many other people are all too willing to take advantage of them by borrowing money and not paying it back, getting behind on child support, or otherwise keeping their money.

I know a woman named Maria who has this problem. Maria is naturally a giving and caring person. If anyone is always ready to fight for the underdog and to rescue people in distress, it's Maria. Unfortunately, her own resources are limited, and sometimes she gets taken advantage of. She works hard at her own small business, and at one time she had her home mortgage almost paid off. Then a close friend needed help. He'd had a streak of bad luck and had no job and no transportation. Most of us would think we'd done our part if we gave him a ride, a few meals, or even $50. Maria loaned him money—more money than she could afford to lose. She bought him a truck and paid for it by refinancing her house. He moved away, took the truck with him, and shows no sign of paying Maria back.

It would be terrible if a bad experience made Maria stop caring for people in need. Her compassionate nature is one thing that makes her special, and the world could use a lot more people like her. However, this isn't the first time Maria has been taken. A few more times like that, and Maria will be the one needing help instead of being able to give it. How can she help people without jeopardizing her own finances?

First, Maria needs to realize that she can't be the one and only solution to anyone's problems. She can't go around adopting full-grown people and their troubles. She should think of nonfinancial ways she can help. Sometimes helping someone find charitable or state aid is more useful than any help a person could ever give on her own. In this case, she could have driven him to appointments, especially job interviews, or helped him figure out where to look for a job. In the meantime, taking him to a local food pantry could have helped him get by. If Maria really felt that her friend needed a truck, she could have bought one and lent it to him. Her biggest mistake was putting it in his name and borrowing the money not against the truck but against her own home. Sure, he promised to make the payments but when he left town with the truck and a clear title, she had no way to stop him.

You may not have refinanced your home to buy someone a truck, but you may remember other debts that people owe you. This would be the ideal time for you to get that money back!

How to get back money someone owes you

Often, friends and relatives who borrow money seem to have perpetual money troubles of their own. Their money troubles become your money troubles when they don't pay you back. If you ever want to see your money again, it pays to know what steps to take.

First, gather your documentation

You'll need canceled checks, promissory notes, rental agreements, and any other evidence of the following:

- Date of loan, sale, or other event

- Dates of any payments made

- Copies of written agreements

- Notes of any verbal agreements

- Interest rate

- Related assets, such as a car

If nothing was ever written down, it's not too late. Tell the person that as part of trying to organize your finances, you need to put things in writing. Most people like to help, and they shouldn't object to getting it on paper. If they say that their word is as good as oak so you don't need to put it on paper . . . then you really need to put it on paper.

Approach the person who owes you money

The hardest part for most people is confronting the person who owes them money. If you lend money to people in need, you are probably a caring, generous person. Unfortunately, as such, you may have a hard time confronting people who test the limits of your generosity.

Always keep your dignity—and theirs. Not only will you feel better if you treat the other person with respect, but you'll be a lot more likely to get your money. Professional collectors say that an understanding, "let's work this out" attitude (with nonpayment not being an option) is much more effective. (Too bad not all collection agencies have figured this out yet.) Hardly anyone borrows money or buys things with bad intentions—it just works out that way all too often!

Think about how you feel when someone calls you about a debt and, in a condescending voice, implies that you're a deadbeat. It's worse if he gets nasty and threatening. You'd be justifiably upset. You may pay the bill if you can, or you may get mad and put it off out of spite. As soon as possible, you may try to forget about the debt and block it from your mind. Caller ID comes in handy! The more caustic and nasty the debt collector gets, the less you want to talk to him. On the other hand, if you owe someone money and he calls and talks reasonably about your situation and how you might pay him back, you are much more likely to respond well.

Remember this when you have to call someone to collect your money. Many people will respond to reason. It may help to remind them in a gentle way that you have bills, too. For example, "I need my money back before my daughter's fall tuition is due," if true, is a hard request to deny. If they are renting from you, remind them that you need the rent to pay the mortgage. People may have no sympathy for a large corporation that they owe money to, but they hate to cause pain to a real person in front of them.

Propose a plan

They may not have the cash right now, but if you wait until they do, it might be the next century. Any payment is better than no payment, and if they can just pay something every payday, they will make progress. Propose setting up a payment schedule. If they bank online, ask if they can set up a regular automatic payment.

Be ready to overcome objections. It's amazing how resourceful you can be when it's your money. They can't deliver the check? What do you know, you'll be in the neighborhood today and you can pick it up. They're trying to sell a motorcycle so they can pay you? Maybe you can take the motorcycle in payment. (Be very, very careful—people tend to inflate the value of things they own.) If they were bluffing and didn't really want to sell the motorcycle, they may decide they can pay you after all!

Charge interest

If they owe you money for more than a short period of time, you should charge interest. For one thing, it's a great motivator for them to pay it off. Why should they pay you, if you don't charge interest and all their other creditors do? Another reason you should charge interest is that with inflation, ten bucks this year isn't really worth ten bucks next year. If you don't charge interest, you're losing money. One way to determine a fair interest rate is to look at what you're paying your creditors in interest. If you're paying 18% on your credit card balances, and someone owes you $1,000 that you could apply to your credit card balances if she paid you, you are paying $15 a month extra interest because of the outstanding loan ($1,000 × 18% divided by 12 months). Isn't it only fair that she pay what it's costing you?

Don't wait!

The longer you wait to collect, the harder it will get, and the less likely it is that you will ever succeed. People have selective memories, and five years later they will likely have completely different stories. They may have made two payments in two years—in their minds they made payments *for* two years! Or, wasn't that a trade for the old couch they gave you? Most people are fairly conscientious, but sometimes to square things up in their own minds, they start rationalizing and rewriting the story. Don't wait until no one can remember the facts and dates clearly.

Also, the longer you wait, the higher the chances are that people who owe you money will leave the state or the country, retire, or go bankrupt. You might still be able to collect after they move or retire, but if they go bankrupt, you're sunk. Many people think that only big credit card companies lose money in bankruptcies. In real life, individuals and small business people are often the hardest hit. I know a small contractor who remodeled a retail store. He worked solely on this store for months, and he paid subcontractors out of his own bank account. He received a few payments, but he was Mr. Nice Guy, waiting patiently while the store owners struggled to make their business succeed so they could pay him. Then they filed for bankruptcy and legally wiped out their debt to him. That's something you never want to experience!

Take legal action

If you can't get a satisfactory response from someone who owes you money, you may need to take legal action. In most cases, that means going to small claims court. You can find many services that will do the paperwork for you, but they often charge 30% to 50% of the total amount—and you still have to supply the information. If you're not afraid of some paperwork, you can do it yourself.

I had a renter once who couldn't seem to remember to pay his rent. Maybe he thought paying the rent was no big deal, but for whatever reason, he got so far behind that it was hard to figure out what month he was paying. When he did pay, I figured there was only a 50% chance the check was good. He was a nice guy; he even sent letters of apology with his late payment sometimes. Apologies don't make my mortgage payment, however.

Eventually my renter moved out, owing several months' rent. He didn't return phone calls. We went to small claims court, which meant that we filled out forms and supplied proof that he owed us money. We paid someone to deliver the documents to him. He never responded, so we won the claim by default and placed a lien on

Definitions

Lien. A legal claim against an asset. If you have a lien against someone's house or car, you get the money she owes you when she sells the house or car—assuming she doesn't have too many other liens in line ahead of you.

Collateral. An asset, such as a car or house, that is pledged to secure a loan or other credit. If credit payments are not made according to the contract, the asset can be seized to pay the debt. Also called security.

some real estate he owned. Some time later, he sold the real estate and the escrow company sent us a check—with interest.

You can go to small claims court and place a *lien* (see sidebar) against someone's house, car, motorcycle, or other valuable assets. You can also use small claims court to garnish someone's wages. For more information, contact the Department of Consumer Affairs for your state.

Next time someone asks you for help

If you are even a little like Maria, you need to be a bit more cautious in your giving. If you can't do it for your own sake, think about your family and friends. You won't be able to help next time if you go overboard now. It's not about being stingy; it's about being more effective in your giving. Here are some things to keep in mind:

- Don't give or lend large amounts of cash. When possible, pay hospital bills and so forth directly.

- Don't give anyone title to something that isn't theirs yet. It's not a matter of not trusting them. It's the way it's done.

- Always, always get loans in writing. When possible, get collateral.

- Be very careful not to gain a dependent. Once you pay a bill, a person finds it easier to ask you to pay the next one. Pretty soon, his bills have become yours. Which brings us to . . .

- Never cosign or guarantee a loan unless you are willing and able to repay the whole loan yourself. You may very well have to—and the other party will still have the car, house, or whatever. I learned this one the hard way myself!

- Don't let the amount anyone owes you get out of hand. The larger the debt, the less likely you are to collect.

Collecting on insurance, wrongful injury, and other judgments

Getting a judgment doesn't mean automatically collecting the money. If you're being ignored by someone you have won a judgment against, you may need to take legal action. If it's a large amount, you will probably need a lawyer, but for smaller cases, you can go to small claims court. The process of collecting from a company is much the same as it is to collect from an individual, described earlier in this chapter. For more information, contact the Department of Consumer Affairs for your state. Look for information for your state on the Internet, or ask your librarian for help.

Should I take an advance from a commercial firm?

If you have won a judgment but have not received the money, or if the money is to be paid to you over a period of time, you can find an advance funding firm that will pay you the money up front. Such firms may even pay you if you have not yet won the case but they are convinced that you will. Of course, this advance funding comes with a cost: A 20% to 30% fee is not uncommon. Some firms also charge interest from the time you get your share until they receive the total. If they charge 5% interest *per month,* as some do, that's over 60% per year!

Job Discrimination and Your Taxes

If you won a legal judgment in a job discrimination suit, you can now deduct your related attorney's fees and court costs on your federal tax return whether you itemize or not. You can deduct up to the amount of income you report from the award, and you do not have to reduce your expenses by 2% of your income, as you do for other miscellaneous deductions.

In most cases, advance funding should be a last resort, simply because it is so expensive. The money you have coming will go faster than you think, and you may regret giving up a large portion of it just to get it faster. For more information, talk to your attorney or paralegal.

Make your ex pay his or her fair share

Trying to live with your children on next to nothing while your children's other parent slides further and further behind in child support is plain wrong. It wrongs not only you but also your children, and in time it wrongs the delinquent parent's relationship with the kids. With the right information, however, you can go after the money you're owed for support.

We all know people, usually women but sometimes men, who are struggling to survive and raise their children with little or no help from their children's other parent. In one afternoon when I was working at a free tax preparation clinic, I met three women who had moved here from other countries with their husbands. All three had children and then were abandoned in a strange country thousands of miles from their extended families. They had no idea how to find financial and legal help, and they were desperate. (Divorce and poverty facts can be found at www.familyfacts.org)

People don't have to come from far away to find themselves in a similar situation. It's not unheard of for someone to come get his kids in a new top-of-the-line pickup, seemingly unembarrassed about being $25,000 behind in child support payments, or for someone to change jobs and move from state to state to keep ahead of her ex's

Statistic

Divorce is the greatest cause of poverty in America.

> ### Statistic
>
> You're not alone. Four out of five noncustodial parents fail to make regular payments.

attempts to collect child support. People even refuse to work or work very little, because they say it would "just go to child support."

One of the best resources that can help you collect child support is the CSE.

What's the CSE?

The federal government created the Child Support Enforcement (CSE) system in 1975 to save taxpayer money. The rationale was that deadbeat parents were getting away with not paying child support, and the American taxpayer was having to pick up the slack through welfare and social service payments.

The CSE was effective enough at helping parents on welfare get child support, and often get off welfare, that people saw that children and parents not on welfare could benefit from the same program. In the 1980s, the program was expanded to help all custodial parents collect child support. Today, CSE program collections amount to billions of dollars per year.

CSE programs can help you find a missing parent and, if necessary, determine paternity. They can establish child support orders and medical support orders. Most notably, they enforce and collect child support, medical support, and spousal support.

Locate a missing parent

In this day of computers and the sharing of information between federal, state, and local agencies, noncustodial parents have to do a lot more than just move to get "lost." They aren't likely to stay lost for long, either: The day they sign up for utilities, get paid, or do almost anything else that requires identification, they are one step closer to being found.

Surprisingly, many noncustodial parents are not that difficult to find. Often only half-hearted attempts, if that, have been made to locate them. The parent raising the kids may be avoiding contact—perhaps out of pride, or sometimes out of fear. The relationship may be so bad that even receiving money from the other parent is more contact than the custodial parent wants. If the parents were never married or if their relationship was a secret, it may be embarrassing as well. The idea of trying to collect can be so traumatic that they would rather get along without it. However, the child's welfare trumps all, and you owe it to your child to collect the support they deserve.

Fortunately, finding that missing parent is easier than ever. Improvements in computerized information sharing, along with changes in state and federal laws, greatly increase your chances of success. The CSE has several tools to help you find the other parent. For example:

The State Licensing Match System and finding noncustodial parents

Many states, such as California, successfully use the State Licensing Match System (SLMS) to track down parents. The first obstacle the CSE often faces in locating a missing parent is that the custodial parent doesn't know the other parent's Social Security number. SLMS

Statistic

More than 70% of the dollars collected in child support come from direct income withholding by employers. In fiscal year 2004, this amounted to approximately $21.9 billion.

Source: http://www.acf.hhs.gov/programs/cse/newhire/employer/private/index.htm

requires driver's license applicants to provide their Social Security numbers along with their names. The CSE can then use this information to help locate delinquent parents.

New Hires and the Federal Parent Locator Service

The Federal Parent Locator Service (FPLS) is a national system that helps states find missing custodial and noncustodial parents. It does this by storing information about employees and information about child support cases and comparing the two.

The information about employees is stored in the National Directory of New Hires (NDNH). As the name implies, when people are hired for a new job, the NDNH collects information about them, including name, Social Security number, and address. It also collects information when someone applies for unemployment benefits and when employers submit quarterly wage reports.

The Federal Case Registry (FCR) stores information about every child support case in every state, along with information about each case. Parents who in the past tried to avoid paying support by moving to another state will find that won't help them much—thanks to the federal registry.

How else does the CSE help collect child support?

The CSE tracks and collects child support. It will arrange to have support payments taken from the other parent's paycheck, for example. For more information, see the CSE Web site at http://www.acf.dhhs.gov/programs/cse.

Should I get a lawyer?

If you have tried other methods without success, or if you simply want to be sure that you get the support your child deserves, consider getting a lawyer. Even with a lawyer, however, you'll need to do your homework. The more documentation and organized records you bring in, the less your lawyer will need to charge you, and the more she will be able to help.

What if my ex says he can't pay because he's on disability or has declared bankruptcy?

Don't give up because your kids' other parent is disabled or is bankrupt. If he is disabled and receives disability checks from the Social Security Administration, his children may qualify for benefits of up to one-half of his full disability amount. For more information, see the Social Security Administration Web site at http://ssa.gov/dibplan/dfamily4.htm.

If he files for bankruptcy and thinks that will get him out of child support payments, he's in for a surprise. Bankruptcy does not get rid of child support—either past or future. In fact, his bankruptcy may benefit you because it may erase some of his other debts, leaving more of his income available for support payments.

What if my kids' other parent dies?

If the other parent dies while your children are still minors, they may qualify for Social Security benefits. If he or she was behind in support payments, you should file with the estate. Support payments are high on the list of debts that must be paid by the estate's assets. Hopefully, the children will also receive something under the will.

Be sure to search for life insurance policies. There is no national database of life insurance policies. The best way to search for them is to make sure the executor of the estate looks for life insurance papers in the deceased person's files. The executor can also scour bank statements and check registers for payments made to life insurance companies. Life insurance companies have no way to automatically know that an insured has died, and every year many policies go unclaimed.

Don't Be Shy

If someone owes you money and isn't paying you, it's time for you to do something about it. Don't be embarrassed to admit that you need the money, and don't be shy or intimidated. You have a right to expect payment, and the longer you wait, the harder it will be. Do the right thing for you and your family: Expect to be treated respectfully, and that means getting paid back in a reasonable manner.

7 Don't Let Uncle Sam Keep Money That's Rightfully Yours

If you're short on money, the last thing you need is for the government to hold on to more of your money than it should. Unfortunately, this happens all too often. You could be running out of money every month at the same time that your employer is taking more tax than necessary out of every paycheck. In addition, you may qualify for advance earned income credit payments that your employer should be adding to your paychecks throughout the year. Chances are that you're not getting the payments if you are entitled to them; only 0.5% of those who qualify for these payments actually receive them.

You could also be missing money the IRS owes you from your prior year tax returns. If you missed some commonly overlooked credits or deductions, you're not too late to get your money back. Another possibility is that you may be able to use current losses to offset income from a prior year so you can actually get a tax refund now. For example, if you have large business losses or if you've been affected by a natural disaster, you may be able to carry your losses back to prior years. It pays to look carefully at all the possibilities; a check from the IRS may be just what you need to get through this rough patch.

Debt and Withholding

The average American family owes over $8,000 in nonmortgage debt. In the meantime, the average American family has over $2,000 more withheld from their paychecks every year than necessary.

Sources: www.cardweb.com/cardtrak/news/2003/march/13a.html
www.irs.gov/taxstats/article/0,,id=102886,00.html

Have the right amount — and no more — withheld from your paychecks

Amy and Andrew seem to be always short of money. Even when they stick to the strictest budget, they can't quite keep up with their expenses. They know that they have about $200 too much taken out of their paychecks every month, but they don't want to give up their once-a-year bonus at tax time. In fact, they count down to the day they can file for their grand and glorious refund. By then, unfortunately, they're in such dire straits that they can't wait the few weeks it takes for the IRS to send them their refund of $2,400. Their tax preparer tells them that they can get a tax refund loan and get that money now! Well, most of their money—what's left after the processing fee.

Now, with the loan, Amy and Andrew have $2,300, which seems like a huge sum of money. Finally, they can do some much needed maintenance on the car and catch up on a few bills. And they've worked hard and deserve a break. The kids want to go to Disneyland. They don't have enough money to pay off the credit cards anyway. Don't they deserve one glorious splurge, one week to have a great time, like everybody else, and not worry about money?

What they don't know is that everybody else—or a good share of them—is also up to their smile-for-the-camera faces in debt, while pretending everything is okay. The average American family owes over $8,000, not counting their home mortgage, and is paying 18%

or so in interest charges on most of that debt. Amy and Andrew will have plenty of company when they get home and face those bills.

Unless they change something soon, this cycle will continue. Every month, they will have just a little bit less than they need to pay their bills, so they will put more and more of their expenses on credit. Maybe they will refinance their house, ensuring that they never make any real progress on paying off their mortgage. Every year, they will get a much-anticipated refund (minus the fees they pay for an instant tax refund loan), and it will be gone before they know it. Their expenses will be higher every month as they spend more and more on interest. What can they do differently?

Amy and Andrew may need to make several changes in their financial habits and in the way they think about their money. The first thing they can do is to stop having too much withheld from their paychecks while they pay beaucoup bucks in interest. Say they have an $8,000 credit card debt, on which they pay only the interest at 18%. That's $120 a month just for interest. If they don't put one more dime on that card, at the end of the year they still owe $8,000. If they get a $2,400 tax refund and apply the whole thing to their credit card debt, they will now owe $5,600. Good for them!

What if they adjust their withholding and use that extra $200 per month to pay down their credit card debt? At the end of the year, they will only owe $5,392. They're $208, or a whole month's payment, ahead!

It's counterproductive to have the government take too much of your money all year while you pay hefty interest fees. The average American family has over $2,000—almost $200 a month—withheld from their paychecks that they don't need to.

"Hang on," you say, "I'd rather have too much taken out than have to pay at the end of the year." If you're so used to getting a refund that it would feel like the Grinch finally stole Christmas if you came out even, then adjust your withholding so you get a small refund—say, two or three hundred bucks. You'll still be able to celebrate, without having lost the use of so much of your money all year.

The High Cost of Overwithholding

If you have $200 too much withheld from your paychecks every month, and you are paying 18% interest on credit card debt, you're paying $208 per year in compounded interest to let Uncle Sam hold your money for you!

How to adjust your withholding

Be very careful when you adjust your withholding. If you have too much income tax withheld, you lose the use of your money for a year. On the other hand, you don't want to have too little withheld and face a big tax bill, possibly with penalties, next year.

Your first goal is to pay enough through withholding that you avoid penalties and interest at tax time. You don't have to worry about these if you have withholding of the so-called safe harbor amount or more. Your safe harbor amount is generally 100% of your tax liability for last year. For example, if you paid $4,000 in income tax last year and you have at least $4,000 withheld from your paycheck this year, you won't owe interest or penalties even if your tax bill this year is substantially more.

The safe harbor amount for high-income taxpayers is slightly higher. If you made over $150,000 in the prior year ($75,000 if you are married filing separately), your safe harbor amount for this year is 110% of the prior year's tax.

If your tax return for last year showed no tax liability, your safe harbor amount is zero, and you are not required to have any federal income tax withheld from your paycheck. (You will still have Social Security and other taxes withheld, of course.)

If you want to pay the minimum amount this year to be sure you won't owe a penalty, you can have your employer withhold the safe harbor amount and then pay the rest when you file your return next year. In theory, this is the best use of your money because you keep it until the last possible moment.

However, this plan could result in an unpleasant shock when you get your tax bill next year. Many people have the best intentions of putting away money for a coming tax bill, and somehow every month slips away without that happening. A safer plan is to project as closely as possible the amount you will owe and have it withheld from your pay throughout the year. Your goal is to either receive a small refund or pay a small amount of tax due when you file your tax return.

When you started working for your employer, you filled out Form W-4 and gave it to someone in personnel. The payroll department uses your filing status (married, single, or "married but withhold at the single rate"), number of exemption allowances, and other information to calculate the amount withheld from your pay. This is where the confusion comes in. Although the number of allowances you should claim is loosely based on how many kids you have, other factors can apply, too. For example, you may need to claim fewer allowances if you make money on the side, or if your spouse also works. However, if you know that you qualify for substantial credits, or if you have big deductions that reduce your taxes, you can claim more allowances to make up for this.

Now you're ready to adjust your income tax withholding. You can do that in three fairly simple steps:

Who Decides?

Myth: Your employer decides how much to withhold from your pay.

Fact: Your employer must withhold exactly the amount shown on federal tax withholding tables, based on your pay, the time period covered, and the information you supplied on Form W-4.

Form **W-4**	**Employee's Withholding Allowance Certificate**	OMB No. 1545-0074
Department of the Treasury Internal Revenue Service	▶ Whether you are entitled to claim a certain number of **allowances** or exemption from withholding is subject to review by the IRS. Your employer may be required to send a copy of this form to the IRS.	**2006**

1	Type or print your first name and middle initial.	Last name			2	Your social security number

	Home address (number and street or rural route)		3	☐ Single ☐ Married ☐ Married, but withhold at higher Single rate.
	City or town, state, and ZIP code			Note. If married, but legally separated, or spouse is a nonresident alien, check the "Single" box.
			4	If your last name differs from that shown on your social security card, check here. You must call 1-800-772-1213 for a new card. ▶ ☐

5	Total number of allowances you are claiming (from line **H** above **or** from the applicable worksheet on page 2)	5	
6	Additional amount, if any, you want withheld from each paycheck	6	$
7	I claim exemption from withholding for 2006, and I certify that I meet **both** of the following conditions for exemption.		
	• Last year I had a right to a refund of **all** federal income tax withheld because I had **no** tax liability **and**		
	• This year I expect a refund of **all** federal income tax withheld because I expect to have **no** tax liability.		
	If you meet both conditions, write "Exempt" here . . . . ▶	7	

Under penalties of perjury, I declare that I have examined this certificate and to the best of my knowledge and belief, it is true, correct, and complete.

Employee's signature
(Form is not valid
unless you sign it.) ▶ _____ Date ▶ _____

8	Employer's name and address (Employer: Complete lines 8 and 10 only if sending to the IRS.)	9	Office code (optional)	10	Employer identification number (EIN)

For Privacy Act and Paperwork Reduction Act Notice, see page 2.	Cat. No. 10220Q	Form **W-4** (2006)

IRS Form W-4, Employee's Withholding Allowance Certificate

1. Find a copy of Form W-4. You can ask someone in your payroll department for a form, or you can download Form W-4 for the current year from the IRS Web site at http://www.irs.gov/formspubs.

2. Figure out how many allowances you should claim and any other changes you should make, and fill out the form. You can use the withholding calculator on the IRS Web site (go to http://www.irs.gov/individuals and click on "IRS Withholding Calculator"). Or you can adjust your Form W-4 by one or two allowances and see how it affects your withholding when you get your next check with the changes. Remember this rule: Fewer allowances mean more tax will be withheld. More allowances mean less tax will be withheld.

3. File the form by giving it to your employer.

Dealing with the Payroll Lady

Dan was getting a sizable refund every year. I convinced him that he should get more money in his paycheck every month, instead of

W-4 Allowances

Myth: You can only claim as many allowances on your Form W-4 as you have kids.

Fact: You can claim as many, or as few, allowances as you need to have the correct amount withheld from your paycheck.

waiting until the end of the year. He didn't want any possibility of having to pay when he filed, so I calculated that he should claim two withholding allowances to end up with a refund of about $300. I filled out a new Form W-4 and told him to take it to the payroll department at work.

Dan came back. "She says I can't do that."

The Payroll Lady had looked over her glasses at Dan as if she had caught him stealing cookies and said, "You can't take more allowances, Dan. I know you don't have any kids." Then she had shooed him back to his cubicle.

It took a lot of persuading to get Dan to face the Payroll Lady again. I told him to tell her that his accountant had filled out this form, and that she had to take it. He did, and she finally relented and accepted the form. For Dan, the result was like getting a raise. He got a little bit more money in every paycheck and a refund of about $300 next time he filed.

Dan still avoids the Payroll Lady, though.

Don't be intimidated by a payroll clerk or anyone else who tries to tell you how to file or says that you can't change your Form W-4. It's your paycheck, and your employer must use the information you provide. You're not cheating; you have the right to adjust your Form W-4 so you have the correct amount withheld.

A better automatic savings plan

What if overwithholding is the only way you seem to be able to put money away? Many people use withholding as an automatic savings plan and swear that it's the only one that works for them, but there are better ways to automatically put money away that get your money started working for you sooner.

One way is to sign up for your employer's 401(k) plan and have a set amount deducted from your pay. By doing that, you'll reduce your taxable income; some employers even make a matching contribution. Or you can have your bank make automatic periodic transfers from your checking account into savings. Another method is to sign up for a plan such as the ones offered at Sharebuilder.com (http://www.sharebuilder.com) through which you can have a certain amount automatically transferred from your checking or savings account every month and invested in stocks, mutual funds, and other investments. The important thing is to get your money working for you now, not next year.

Earned Income Credit

Jeanette had just been evicted from her apartment and was carrying her valuables around in her car. The fact that she had everything with her turned out to be an incredible stroke of luck, because as we stood by her car talking, I noticed file folders marked TAXES. I wondered if she was getting the earned income credit (EIC) and if she should be getting a portion of the credit added to each of her paychecks, so I asked to see her returns.

I knew Jeanette had two children living with her, so I asked her why her EIC form only showed one. She said that she had an agreement with her ex that he could take a dependency exemption for one of the kids. I told her that the EIC doesn't have anything to do with who is taking the dependency exemption. If your children under age eighteen (or under age twenty-four if they're going to school full time) live with you more than half the year, you can claim them for the EIC credit. The difference even one child makes when calculating the EIC can be substantial!

I didn't want to get Jeanette's hopes up, so I studied her tax returns from the last few years before I said anything. When I was absolutely sure, I told her to file amended returns for three years. She wondered if it would be worth the trouble. I assured her that her refund would be substantial. In fact, it would be enough to get her back on her feet financially.

Jeanette filed an amended return for the preceding three years and got over $4,000 back from Uncle Sam. If only we could have gone back ten years to the time of her divorce! Unfortunately, taxpayers can only amend returns and get refunds for three years back.

Jeanette took that $4,000 and got into a new apartment. She used it to pay her rent ahead, so she and her kids could feel secure about having a place to live.

Jeanette had at least been getting a partial EIC all those years. Many taxpayers who should get the EIC don't, either because they don't understand it or because they think it's too hard to claim. Even though the EIC has been around since 1975, people still find it difficult to believe that the IRS wants to give them back more money than they had withheld from their paychecks.

It's true, though. The EIC was created to help offset the burden of Social Security taxes on low-income taxpayers, and over the years it has been expanded as a way to help those taxpayers and encourage them to work. It provides more than $20 billion in assistance per year. Yet about 25% of the 17.2 million families eligible for the credit never claim it. That's over 4 million families missing out on thousands of much-needed dollars each.*

If your family might be one of those, take the time to complete the following worksheet.

Earned Income Credit Worksheet

To qualify for the earned income credit, you must be able to answer yes to all of the following questions:

---

*U.S. General Accounting Office 2002

- Do you have earned income—taxable or nontaxable—such as wages, tips, self-employment income, union strike benefits, housing allowances, combat zone pay, or any other compensation for your work?

- Is your investment income (for 2005) no more than $2,700? Investment income includes taxable and tax-exempt interest, dividends, net capital gains, and other income from your investments.

- Do you use a filing status other than "married filing separately"?

- Do you, your spouse, and any children you are claiming for the EIC have Social Security numbers?

If you have one or more qualifying children, you must also be able to answer yes to the following questions:

- Is your earned income, such as wages and tips, less than $31,030 ($33,030 if you file jointly) if you have only one qualifying child, or less than $35,263 ($37,263 if you file jointly) if you have more than one qualifying child?

- Is each child you are claiming for the EIC credit your relative, adopted child, or foster child who lived in your home for more than six months of the year? (Any child you care for as your own is considered a foster child.)

- Is the child under age 19 or a full-time student under age 24 at the end of the year, or any age and totally and permanently disabled?

- If two people qualify to claim a child for the EIC, are you the person with the higher income?

If you do not have qualifying children, you may qualify for the EIC if you can answer yes to the following questions:

- Are you at least age twenty-five, but under age sixty-five, at the end of the year? (If you are married, only one of you must meet this requirement.)

- Are your earned income and modified adjusted gross income both less than $11,750 ($13,750 if you file jointly)?

- Are neither you nor your spouse qualified to be claimed as a dependent on anyone else's return?

- Is your main home in the United States for more than six months of the year?

In addition, you must be able to answer no to all of the following questions whether or not you have children:

- Are you a qualifying child for someone else who is claiming the earned income credit?

- Are you filing Form 2555, Foreign Earned Income, to claim the foreign income exclusion?

- Are you a nonresident alien for any part of the year (unless you are married to a U.S. citizen or resident and elect to be taxed as a U.S. resident all year)?

Your EIC amount is determined from the IRS tables, based on your earned income and how many kids you have, if any. If you have no children, you may receive up to $399 (in 2005). If you have children, you may receive much more—up to $2,662 if you have one child, and up to $4,400 if you have more than one child.

For more information about the EIC, and help with calculating your earned income, including numbers for the current year, see Publication 596, *Earned Income Credit (EIC)*, on the IRS Web site at http://www.irs.gov/publications/p596/index.html.

Advance earned income credit

If you qualify for the earned income credit and you have at least one child, you generally don't have to wait until you file your tax return to receive your credit. You can start getting EIC payments in your next paycheck. It's remarkable how few taxpayers take advantage of the advance payments. In 1989, for example, only about 40,000 families received advance payments, less than 0.5% of those eligible.

Signing up to get the advance earned income credit is easy. Form W-5 is a short, simple form. You can file it with your employer and start getting more money in every paycheck.

You can ask for Form W-5 at work, or you can download it from the IRS Web site at http://www.irs.gov/formspubs/lists/0,,id=97817,00 .html. You must sign up for the advance EIC again every year that you qualify.

If you receive EIC advance payments, your employer will include them in Box 9 of your Form W-2 at the end of the year, and you must report them on your tax return.

The advance payments you receive will reduce your refund. If you receive too much in credits, you may have to repay some. This is unlikely, however, because the advance credit is calculated to give you only about 60% of the total EIC credit you will receive for the year. Your situation would have to change dramatically for you to have to make a repayment.

.... Detach here ....

Form **W-5**	**Earned Income Credit Advance Payment Certificate**	OMB No. 1545-0074
Department of the Treasury Internal Revenue Service	▶ Use the current year's certificate only. ▶ Give this certificate to your employer. ▶ This certificate expires on December 31, 2006.	2006

Print or type your full name	Your social security number

Note. *If you get advance payments of the earned income credit for 2006, you* **must** *file a 2006 federal income tax return. To get advance payments, you* **must** *have a qualifying child and your filing status must be any status* **except** *married filing a separate return.*

1   I expect to have a qualifying child and be able to claim the earned income credit for 2006 using that child. I do not have
    another Form W-5 in effect with any other current employer, and I choose to get advance EIC payments . . . .   ☐ **Yes** ☐ **No**
2   Check the box that shows your expected filing status for 2006:
    ☐ Single, head of household, or qualifying widow(er)   ☐ Married filing jointly
3   If you are married, does your spouse have a Form W-5 in effect for 2006 with any employer?. . . . .   ☐ **Yes** ☐ **No**

Under penalties of perjury, I declare that the information I have furnished above is, to the best of my knowledge, true, correct, and complete.

Signature ▶   Date ▶

Cat. No. 10227P

IRS Form W-5, *Earned Income Credit Advance Payment Certificate*

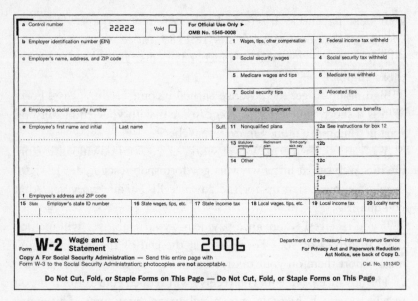

IRS Form W-2, Wage and Tax Statement

Finding missed deductions and credits from prior years' returns

Ann did the best she could filing her returns. As a busy professional and mother, she gathered up receipts as well as she could and took them to her accountant. He didn't ask many questions. In fact, that was one thing she liked about this accountant: He just took her stacks of statements and receipts and produced a tax return for her to sign. She usually got a small tax refund, so all was well.

Then Ann got downsized, along with thousands of other high-tech workers who all typed up their résumés at once and descended on the employment agencies. By the time Ann realized that it was going to take a while to find another job, she was in trouble financially. She started to wonder about her hastily prepared tax returns. If only she had paid better attention.

I suggested to Ann that it might not be too late to take another look at the returns for the last three years and see if she could honestly get something back from Uncle Sam.

We didn't find anything earthshaking on Ann's returns, but I noticed that some income on her Form W-4 was included twice on her return—as wages and also as a separate item. She remembered some noncash charitable contributions, including mileage for volunteer work she had done. A few more changes, and Ann filed Form 1040X to get back money that was rightfully hers. It was definitely worth the trouble.

It may be very well worth your time and effort to carefully go over your tax returns for the last three years. (You generally can't go back further than that.)

Pay special attention to these items that are commonly overlooked:

- **Social Security tax withheld.** If you work for more than one employer, you may have had too much Social Security tax withheld. Add up the "Social Security tax withheld" amounts on your Form W-2s to see if you had more than $5,840.40 (in 2006) withheld in one year.

- **Noncash charitable contributions.** You can deduct the fair market value of most items, such as household goods, vehicles, and clothing, that you donate to qualified organizations. You cannot take a deduction for anything you donate to individuals.

- **Education credits or deductions.** Take the education credits, known as the Hope Credit or the Lifetime Learning Credit, if you qualify. Otherwise, you can generally take a deduction for education expenses whether or not you itemize, for tax years 2002 through 2005. This tax break is expected to be extended.

- **Sales tax deduction.** Starting in 2005, you can deduct either your state income tax or an amount for state sales tax. You must choose one or the other; you cannot deduct both. This tax break is also expected to be extended.

- **Child-care credit.** If you paid someone to take care of your child or other dependent so you could work, you may be able to take a credit of up to $2,100 (in 2004).

- **Foreign tax credit.** You may not have even known that you paid foreign tax, but if you invest in mutual funds, there's a good chance that you did. You may be able to take a credit for foreign taxes you paid. Check your brokerage statements for amounts labeled "Foreign tax paid."

- **Volunteer expenses.** If you do volunteer work for a qualified charitable organization, you can deduct your expenses, including expenses for transportation and supplies. You cannot deduct anything for your time spent as a volunteer.

- **Bad debt.** If you loaned someone a substantial amount of money and were never repaid, you may qualify for a deduction in the year the debt became worthless.

How to change your tax returns from prior years

If you need to change your tax return for a prior year, you must file a Form 1040X, Amended U.S. Individual Income Tax Return. Form 1040X looks nothing like an original Form 1040, U.S. Individual Income Tax Return. Instead, it is a summary sheet that shows the amounts you originally reported, increases or decreases in those amounts, and the corrected amounts. You can also use it to report other changes, such as changes in your filing status.

In general, you must file Form 1040X by the *later* of these dates: three years after the date you filed the original return (or the deadline for the return if you filed it early), or two years after the date you paid the tax. You have seven years after the due date of the return to file a Form 1040X because a debt someone owed you became uncollectible or stock became worthless.

Form **1040X**
(Rev. November 2005)

Department of the Treasury—Internal Revenue Service

Amended U.S. Individual Income Tax Return

▶ See separate instructions.

OMB No. 1545-0074

This return is for calendar year ▶ _____ , or fiscal year ended ▶ _____

Please print or type

| Your first name and initial | Last name | Your social security number |
| If a joint return, spouse's first name and initial | Last name | Spouse's social security number |

Home address (no. and street) or P.O. box if mail is not delivered to your home | Apt. no. | Phone number ( )

City, town or post office, state, and ZIP code. If you have a foreign address, see page 2 of the instructions. | For Paperwork Reduction Act Notice, see page 6.

A If the address shown above is different from that shown on your last return filed with the IRS and you would like us to change it, check here . . . . ▶ ☐

B Filing status. Be sure to complete this line. **Note.** You cannot change from joint to separate returns after the due date.

On original return ▶ ☐ Single ☐ Married filing jointly ☐ Married filing separately ☐ Head of household ☐ Qualifying widow(er)

On this return ▶ ☐ Single ☐ Married filing jointly ☐ Married filing separately ☐ Head of household* ☐ Qualifying widow(er)

* If the qualifying person is a child but not your dependent, see page 2 of the instructions.

Use Part II on the back to explain any changes

Income and Deductions (see instructions)		A. Original amount or as previously adjusted (see page 3)	B. Net change—amount of increase or (decrease)—explain in Part II	C. Correct amount
1 Adjusted gross income (see page 3)	**1**			
2 Itemized deductions or standard deduction (see page 3). .	**2**			
3 Subtract line 2 from line 1	**3**			
4 Exemptions. If changing, fill in Parts I and II on the back (see page 3)	**4**			
5 Taxable income. Subtract line 4 from line 3	**5**			
6 Tax (see page 4). Method used in col. C _____	**6**			
7 Credits (see page 4)	**7**			
8 Subtract line 7 from line 6. Enter the result but not less than zero .	**8**			
9 Other taxes (see page 4)	**9**			
10 Total tax. Add lines 8 and 9	**10**			
11 Federal income tax withheld and excess social security and tier 1 RRTA tax withheld. If changing, see page 4 . . .	**11**			
12 Estimated tax payments, including amount applied from prior year's return	**12**			
13 Earned income credit (EIC)	**13**			
14 Additional child tax credit from Form 8812	**14**			
15 Credits from Form 2439, Form 4136, or Form 8885 . .	**15**			
16 Amount paid with request for extension of time to file (see page 4)				**16**
17 Amount of tax paid with original return plus additional tax paid after it was filed				**17**
18 Total payments. Add lines 11 through 17 in column C				**18**

Refund or Amount You Owe

19 Overpayment, if any, as shown on original return or as previously adjusted by the IRS		**19**
20 Subtract line 19 from line 18 (see page 5)		**20**
21 **Amount you owe.** If line 10, column C, is more than line 20, enter the difference and see page 5 .		**21**
22 If line 10, column C, is less than line 20, enter the difference		**22**
23 Amount of line 22 you want **refunded to you**		**23**
24 Amount of line 22 you want **applied to your** _____ **estimated tax**	**24**	

Sign Here
Joint return?
See page 2.
Keep a copy for your records.

Under penalties of perjury, I declare that I have filed an original return and that I have examined this amended return, including accompanying schedules and statements, and to the best of my knowledge and belief, this amended return is true, correct, and complete. Declaration of preparer (other than taxpayer) is based on all information of which the preparer has any knowledge.

▶ Your signature | Date | ▶ Spouse's signature. If a joint return, **both** must sign. | Date

Paid Preparer's Use Only

Preparer's signature ▶		Date	Check if self-employed ☐	Preparer's SSN or PTIN
Firm's name (or yours if self-employed), address, and ZIP code ▶			EIN	
			Phone no. ( )	

Cat. No. 11360L

Form **1040X** (Rev. 11-2005)

IRS Form 1040X, Amended U.S. Individual Income Tax Return, top portion shown

If you live in a state with state income tax, don't forget to amend your state returns, too.

Carry back a net operating loss

If your income this year is less than your deductions on your Form 1040, you may have a net operating loss (NOL) that you can apply against your income in the prior two years and get back some of the tax you paid. A loss from your trade or business, job-related deductions, or losses from a casualty or theft are the only things that can generate an NOL.

To carry back an NOL, you can either file an amended return (Form 1040X) for the year to which you carry back the loss, or you can file Form 1045, Application for Tentative Refund. You can carry any remaining NOL forward up to twenty years, until it is used up.

Alternatively, you can elect to *only* carry an NOL forward. You will get the benefit sooner by carrying it back, unless you paid little or no tax in the prior two years. In that case, you generally receive a greater tax benefit by electing to only carry the loss forward. You must attach this election to your return in the year you had the loss. You must file the election within six months of the original due date of your return, and you cannot change your mind once you have filed.

Deduct a casualty loss from a disaster in a presidentially declared disaster area

You can generally only deduct casualty losses that do not result in an NOL in the year the casualty occurred. However, if you have a deductible loss from a disaster in a presidentially declared disaster area, you can deduct that loss on your tax return for the year before the year of the casualty. This allows you to get a refund sooner. Deducting the loss from the prior year will be especially beneficial to you if your income was higher in that year.

If you have already filed your return for the preceding year, you can claim the loss in that year by filing an amended return on Form 1040X. You generally have until the due date of the current year's return (usually April 15) to decide if you want to take the deduction in the year of the disaster or in the prior year.

I filed Form 1040X, now where's my refund?

If you found some items you had missed on your tax returns and filed Form 1040X, now comes the hard part: waiting for your refund. Refunds from Form 1040X can take a bit longer than refunds on original tax returns. You will most likely get your refund in one to three months. If you haven't received anything twenty-eight days after you mail the form, you can go to the IRS Web site at http://www.irs.gov/individuals and click on "Where's My Refund?" to check the status of your tax return and refund.

It's Your Money

When it comes to taxes, don't pay any more or any sooner than you are required to, and be sure to take advantage of programs like the earned income credit if you qualify. Tax benefits like these were designed to help people like you, and they may provide just the help you need to get through difficult financial times.

8 Borrow to Get Through Hard Times

Get a new loan or
credit card, or refinance
your house

Getting another loan or credit card might seem counterproductive when you're already in debt. After all, shouldn't you be getting rid of debt, not adding to it? In fact, getting one more loan, if you're not careful, can be a short-term fix with an unbearable long-term price. Some new loans come with all kinds of unpleasant surprises, like rising interest rates and a multitude of fees. Plus, if the underlying reasons for your money troubles don't change, you'll be right back looking for another loan before you know it.

If you plan it right, however, getting a new loan can be part of a smart strategy for surviving a financial crisis and getting back on track. For example, a new loan might buy you some time until you land a better-paying job. If you are paying high interest rates and fees on several loans and credit cards, getting a loan with lower rates can be a smart move—*if* you get rid of the old cards and don't max them out again.

Two couples—two different results

The Walters and the Austens were both entirely dependent on income from their small businesses. Both businesses hit hard times, and the bills piled up. Both couples maxed out their credit cards and cut expenses to the minimum, but still they couldn't keep up. They got behind on their taxes. With interest rates at a historic low, refinancing seemed like a good idea.

The Walters were amazed at how much their house had gone up in value over the last few years. They were able to refinance, pay all their bills and taxes, and even fly to Tahoe for the weekend. With their credit history, they paid hefty refinancing fees and didn't qualify for the low interest rates they'd seen advertised. Even so, with bills paid and cash in their pockets, they at least had a new start.

Unfortunately for the Walters, their business problems continued. Their business revenue wasn't enough to cover payroll and office expenses, and soon they were behind again. By now their credit was so bad that they had to pay twice the going mortgage interest rate, but they didn't see much of a choice. Property values were still rising, fortunately, so they refinanced again. A larger mortgage at a scandalous interest rate meant huge payments they couldn't handle, and eventually the Walters lost the home that they had lived in for thirty years—about the time they should have been able to retire.

When the Austens' business hit a slump, they, too, worked all the harder and cut expenses. Soon they realized that they had a choice: They could sell their house, use the money to pay bills and overdue taxes, and move into an apartment, or they could refinance. The Austens had been careful to make the minimum payments on their credit cards, so they qualified for a new mortgage at a competitive rate. They refinanced for no more than necessary, so the mortgage payments were not much different than before. Their business still has its ups and downs, but the Austens still own their home and are still building up equity in it.

Refinancing turned out to be a useful tool for the Austens, while it led to financial disaster for the Walters. What made the difference? The Austens took a more long-term view. They paid careful attention to what the loan was actually costing them. They didn't see refinancing as a source of free money, and they didn't refinance repeatedly, increasing the amount they owed every time. The Walters, however, became credit and refinancing junkies. They saw refinancing as the fix for their money woes. As they discovered, refinancing never solves financial problems by itself—there's that problem of having to pay it back.

Are you a credit or refinancing junkie?

Do any of these warning signs apply to you?

- You've refinanced your home two or more times, increasing the amount you owe each time.

- You see extra cash from refinancing or from a new credit card as free money.

- You always refinance to the maximum percentage allowed.

- You quickly reach the maximum credit limit whenever you get a new credit card.

- When you refinance, you don't pay much attention to total fees or the new balance you will owe on your house. All that matters is how much cash you get and your monthly payments.

- You're getting closer to retirement age, but you're not building equity in your home.

If even one of these signs applies, you may be in danger of relying too much on borrowing to solve your problems. The best way to avoid a destructive borrower's mentality is to always think about your total financial picture. What matters is what you own versus what you owe—and when you remember that, you won't want to pay thousands of dollars to refinance your home again this year. You'll view a high credit limit on a new card with distrust; you may even call and request that the credit limit be lowered. When you are forced to rely on borrowing to get through a temporary money crisis, you'll immediately be looking for ways to change your monthly income and expenses so it stays a temporary crisis—not a way of life.

When can borrowing help you get through a financial crisis?

Borrowing isn't always bad! If you do it right, it can even help you get out of debt. New borrowing might be a good idea if:

- You can reduce your interest rate—and therefore your monthly interest expense—significantly.

- The new loan makes it possible for you to make more progress on paying off your balance.

- The interest rate can't spike unexpectedly, as with some adjustable rate mortgages (ARMs) or teaser-rate credit cards.

- It doesn't cost more than it's worth. It's no use spending thousands to refinance and lower your monthly payment by a couple of hundred dollars a month.

- It's part of a realistic overall plan to get out of debt.

- You're in a sudden, unavoidable money squeeze, and borrowing is your only option. In this case, immediately make plans to improve your financial situation so you won't be in this vulnerable position again.

Should you refinance?

Before you choose the best refinancing deal for your home, you need to decide how long you intend to live in your home. If the answer is two years or less, it's probably not worth it. By the time you go to all the trouble and expense of getting refinanced and paying refinancing fees, you aren't likely to come out ahead.

Refinancing costs more than many ads would have you believe. Many places advertise low or even no closing fees, but that doesn't mean it won't cost you anything. You almost always have to pay for an appraisal, which can be several hundred dollars. There's the loan origination fee, which can be 1% of the loan. On a $200,000 mortgage, that's $2,000. It can be a rude surprise when you close on your new loan to discover how much a "no closing fees" loan really costs!

Then there are points.

What are points?

Points are an additional amount you pay when you take out a mortgage, generally in exchange for a lower interest rate. The more points you pay, the lower your rate. Each point is 1% of the mortgage. The longer you intend to stay in a house, the more you should be willing to pay in points.

Is refinancing worth it?

Before you sign up for a new loan, ask for the amount of your new payments (not including insurance and property taxes) and an estimate of your total cost to refinance. Compare the payments you would make under a new mortgage with your current payments. If it looks like you can save a significant amount every month, check one more thing: How long will it take for you to break even?

Divide the total cost of refinancing by the amount you will save every month. For example, if it will cost you $3,000 to refinance, and you will save $300 per month, you will break even in ten months ($3,000 divided by $300). If you are sure you will live in this house for several years, go ahead and refinance.

You can use the "Is Refinancing Worth It?" online calculator at HelpICantPayMyBills.net to estimate your refinancing costs and determine how long it will take you to break even.

Finding a good credit card deal

When you're desperate for cash and you get mail promising instant credit, or even checks that you can use like cash, it's awfully tempting to take one without shopping around. After all, credit cards from major banks should be competitive, right?

Perhaps if everyone shopped around, the rates would be more comparable. In the Internet age, when you can go online and compare hundreds of different cards, you would think that competition would force financial institutions to offer customers their best deal. Instead, you find that one card charges high annual fees and interest rates, while another offers bonus points that can help pay for anything from airline tickets to toys. What gives? Are the high-fee, high-interest cards only for people who aren't paying attention?

One reason card deals vary is that one card will never be the best deal for everyone. If you pay your card off every month, you don't care what the interest rate is. You'd rather have a card with no annual fee, and maybe some perks like department store certificates every time you spend a certain amount. If you carry a balance, especially if you intend to transfer balances over from other cards, the interest rate is the most important thing.

Interest rates can be deceiving, however. Credit card ads often say things like "0% interest" in huge type, and then, in tiny little print that no one over forty can read without a magnifying glass, they tell you that the interest rate can change in three months, or if you are ever late, or if they feel like it. That's the bad thing about using credit cards as loans: You are at their mercy if you carry a balance that you cannot pay off. Once you have a balance, they can raise the rate, and you might not even notice. If the interest rate goes up, and you can't pay it off or transfer it to another card, you're stuck.

One trick people try is hopping from one low-introductory-rate credit card to another. They get a new card and use the free checks to transfer all their other, high-interest card debt to the new card. When the interest rate rises, they look for another card with a low intro rate and transfer all their debt again. While taking advantage of those low rates is an excellent idea if you can use the interest savings to quickly pay down your debt, hopping from one card to another indefinitely is not a long-term solution. For one thing, applying for new credit cards every three months doesn't look good on your credit report. For another thing, it's all too easy to accumulate more and more debt as you go, or to forget to keep tabs on the interest rate on your new card.

Where to look for loans

It's tempting to take advantage of the loans and credit offers that you see all around you. They even come to your mailbox. Credit card offers in the mail, refinancing offers in your e-mail in-box—they make it look so easy. They might not be your best deal, however.

I wouldn't do business with a company that sends out unsolicited e-mail—the dreaded spam. In the age of identity theft, who would send these people personal financial information?

Next in likely loan and credit sources is the junk mail in your physical mailbox. At least, most of these are from real banks. You may get several offers a week, and some of them may sound good. Before you pick the best out of half a dozen, however, consider that there are hundreds of options out there. Why pick from six?

Compare hundreds of top-rated credit cards or mortgages

You can find the best deals by going to a Web site such as Bankrate .com (www.bankrate.com) and entering the criteria most important to you. You can choose from hundreds of credit card and mortgage deals from across the country. Look for:

- **No annual fee.** If you can choose between a card with a fee and one without, why would you pay a fee? Only pay annual fees if they are outweighed by other benefits.

- **Low interest rates.** If you carry a balance, even a few points make a big difference. Read the fine print here: How long does it stay at this rate? Can it go up at any time without notice?

- **Customer satisfaction rating.** How happy are other customers? If the company's customer service is terrible, you want to know.

- **Perks!** If you need to use a credit card, why not choose one that gives you airline miles, free coffee, or credits toward toys?

Credit unions

If you belong to a credit union or can join one, you may find your best deal there. Credit unions are not-for-profit, which means they can pass their savings on to you. Don't take it for granted, however; do your comparison shopping carefully.

Personal loans

Don't overlook personal loans. When you borrow directly from someone, you are bypassing the bank and the profit it must make to stay in business. You may be able to pay someone a rate of interest that's higher than he can get from the bank yet lower than the rate you would pay on a loan or credit card. You both win—if you pay a fair interest rate and you keep your end of the deal. If the individual is very nice and says you don't need to pay interest, pay it anyway. It's the right thing to do.

We borrowed part of our down payment from a relative when we bought a house. With her help, we were able to make a large enough down payment to avoid paying private mortgage insurance (PMI). We paid her an interest rate halfway between the going mortgage rate and the rate she could get on a certificate of deposit (CD) at the bank. She didn't want monthly payments, so we paid her back when we sold the house a few years later. It worked out well for both of us.

If you take out a personal loan, make it official. Put it in writing, and include the amount and date of the loan, the interest rate, and the expected payback schedule. You can use the worksheet from HelpICantPayMyBills.net to plan a payment schedule and to calculate the interest and principal portions of each payment and the amount you still owe.

CAUTION: Never borrow money from friends and family that you might not be able to repay. It isn't fair to them, and you'll be embarrassed and feel terrible. You may lose your friendship forever. If you are ever forced into bankruptcy, they may never be paid. Many people say, "Even if I go bankrupt, I'll pay you back." Very few follow through.

Where not to borrow money

Stay away from pawn shops, payday advance centers, and other short-term loan services. If you need these loans, you can't afford the fees and interest rates they charge.

9 Second Jobs and Temporary Work

Rowing harder for a while
can pay off

Sometimes when you need more money, the solution is simply to make more of it. When you're short on money, every extra dollar counts. When my daughter was a baby and my finances had totally tanked, I used to make grocery money watching other people's kids. Back then, the going rate for child care was $1 per hour. I'd have to watch a colicky baby for a week to buy a couple of bags of groceries. I made that money go a long way! Forty bucks doesn't sound like much, but the difference between that and nothing is huge when you're out of milk.

You can find something that pays better than I did back then. Whether you need a second source of income or temporary work to tide you over while you're unemployed, don't shortchange yourself by thinking that you're overqualified for some jobs or not good enough for others. Try to open your eyes to all the possibilities.

The hardest obstacle to overcome can be our pride. Like the young lawyer who ran an ice cream truck in another town on weekends—so the law firm's clients wouldn't see him tootling around to a tinny rendition of "The Entertainer" on Saturdays—we may have face to save. But what are we really hiding? If someone loses her job, does hiding that fact help her find a new one? Will friends think less of someone if they see him busing tables or sweeping the food court?

Maybe we take ourselves too seriously. Other people hit hard times, too. If people see us working hard to make ends meet, not at all embarrassed and hopefully even in good humor, they may find it easier to do the same someday. They may even think more highly of us, as in, "That Dave pitched right in—he wasn't afraid to work." People are more impressed by those who aren't afraid to pitch in than they are by those who think they are too good for manual labor. I knew a man who owned several retirement centers and other businesses. If he stopped by and found they were short a dishwasher, he took off his suit jacket and scrubbed pots and pans. Did people think less of him for getting his hands soapy? Far from it!

That brings up the next fear: We might be afraid that the secondary or temporary job a few rungs lower on the ladder isn't that easy. It may turn out that we've had it rather cushy for a few years. We might not be able to keep up with the younger people. The truth is that many jobs—especially entry-level ones—are extremely demanding. You may be on your feet all day, have a lot to keep track of, and have several people telling you what to do all at once. On the other hand, you may be surprised at what you can do. You may get a great sense of accomplishment and pride when you find that you can do the job well.

Is there something you've always wanted to try but haven't had a chance to? A friend of mine always jokes, when his job gets tough, "I think I'll just go sell ladies' shoes." A Christmas season in a department store might cure him of that idea—or he might have a blast. Maybe you'd like to try something that demands creativity, gets you outdoors, or involves working with children or the elderly. Now's your chance.

Where to find secondary or temporary work

If you will be actively seeking a permanent position and need the flexibility to go to interviews, it's best to find a job where you can be honest about your intentions. If you have to hide your job-seeking activities and make excuses every time you have an interview, you only add to your stress. Besides, job hunting in secret is hardly the best strategy!

If you're looking for a temporary full-time or secondary job, try a temporary agency. These places aren't what they used to be. When I was working my way through college, being a Kelly Girl meant going around to different offices helping them catch up on clerical work or filling in when someone was on vacation. Most jobs were short—some only a few days—and there was seldom any chance of being hired on a permanent basis. That's not the way it works anymore.

Today, not only has the name "Kelly Girl" gone out of style (it's now Kelly Services), but today's temporary agencies employ people of all skill levels for a wide range of jobs. Job contracts often last for three months and can be extended. Many professionals work for "temporary" agencies on a permanent basis, enjoying the freedom of being able to take assignments as they please. They are known as "contractors" at their place of employment, because they work on contract through the agency. Some even work at the same company where they were formerly employed as permanent employees. Far from being unhappy, most contractors I have known are happy with this arrangement. They point out that they now get paid for every hour they work, their job is much more clearly defined, and they aren't as involved in office politics. Many of them like contracting so well that they wouldn't have it any other way.

If you can find a temporary job in your field or close to it, you might even be on your way to a permanent position. Many businesses now use temporary services as a "try before you buy" hiring method. You and the business both get to check each other out for a period of time. If you work out really well, or even turn out to be indispensable, you may be offered a permanent position. The company generally pays a fee to the agency for taking you out of circulation.

So many jobs are now available on a temporary basis that it would be impossible to make even a partial list of them. Some of the most common temporary positions, however, include these:

- Substitute teacher

- Computer programmer

- Administrative assistant

- Data entry clerk

- Writer and editor

- Graphic artist

It might be easier to list the jobs that are not available on a temporary basis! The chances are very good that you can find temporary work of some kind. It may be a temporary adventure, or it may turn into a new job or career. You never know until you try it.

Seasonal work

Marsha was a manager in the construction industry until she and many of her coworkers were unexpectedly laid off. She found herself with nothing to fall back on, lots of bills, and two kids to support—and it was Christmastime. The local department stores were hiring extra seasonal help, so she applied. She explained in her interview that she was looking for a permanent job in her field, and the store agreed to let her take time off for interviews. The work was hectic.

She had to get used to being trained by girls her daughter's age, and she discovered how it feels to deal with cranky customers. On the upside, she made enough to pay some bills, and she proved to herself that she could do it. She eventually found another job in management, but her Christmas season in retail helped her make it through a tough spot. Her learning experience there also became a source of interesting and funny stories—at least now that they're in the past.

The Christmas shopping season is an obvious time to look for seasonal work. Besides retail stores, restaurants, UPS, security companies, and the Post Office all hire extra people in November and December. Other seasons offer opportunities as well. Consider:

- Tax preparation (January through April)

- Ski instruction (winter)

- Any winter resort work, from café to ski check-ins

- Lifeguarding (summer)

- Farm work (summer)

- Youth camp jobs (summer)

- Yard work (spring, summer, fall)

- Forest Service jobs (summer)

Day labor agencies

The true temporary agencies of today, day labor agencies find work for you for today—and they generally pay you today, too. If the cupboards are bare and the gas tank is nearly empty, you might check it out. The largest day labor agency in the United States is Labor Ready, which hires people for everything from food service and warehouse work to unskilled construction. They hire both young and more experienced workers. Some jobs, such as furniture moving, require heavy lifting, but there are also less physical jobs, such as answering the phones or filing. Some day labor agencies require you to come first thing in the morning to see if any employers need workers; others take your information and call you when you are needed.

For more information, see the Labor Ready Web site at www. laborready.com or contact a day labor agency in your area.

Your own business

One of the best ways to make extra money is to start your own home-based business. When you are short of money, a home-based business is ideal because your start-up cost should be relatively low. In fact, some home-based businesses cost nothing or almost nothing to start.

Home-based businesses have gotten a bad name because so many of the ideas for starting them you see advertised turn out to be either unworkable or outright scams. The easiest way to avoid getting ripped off by these schemes and finding yourself worse off than before is to make sure that your home-based business idea has all the components of any good business idea:

- **A great product or service that people need or want.** It won't work if people don't buy it or if the market is already flooded.

- **A realistic plan for selling the product or service.** Ask yourself: How will people who need your product or service find it? How would you find it if you wanted to buy it?

- **A workable business plan.** If you are making something to sell, calculate the cost and time to make each item, and be sure it's worth it. Don't forget to include your sales expense and time.

- **A business that doesn't compete with labor in China.** Service-based businesses are often a better idea than sewing, crafts, or other manufacturing businesses because retailers can buy goods made overseas so cheaply. They can't have overseas workers clean offices, repair cars, or watch the children in your neighborhood, however.

You can start a business yourself. You don't have to respond to "home-based business" ads. You probably don't need to pay for a franchise. Just find a need and fill it—and you'll be on your way to making extra money, or even a good income, before you know it.

Consider these proven home-based business ideas. Some require more special skills or experience than others. Think about the skills you have and how you will be able to help people. Helping people is what business is all about.

- Bookkeeping

- Buying cars wholesale or at auctions and reselling them

- Buying things in bulk and reselling them online

- Catering

- Child care (day, after-school, or drop-in)

- Clothing alterations and repairs

- Computer programming

- Computer repair and consulting

- Computer tutoring

- Driveway resealing

- Editing

- Errand running

- Hauling (debris, supplies)

- Home inspection

- Home repair

Help! I Can't Pay My Bills

- Housecleaning

- Housepainting

- Language translating

- Locksmithing

- Medical billing (don't pay for an expensive franchise—you don't need it!)

- Medical transcription

- Moving help

- Music lessons

- Office cleaning (ideal after-hours job)

- Party planning

- Pet sitting

- Piano tuning

- Plant caretaking

- Proofreading

- Real estate appraisal

- Résumé writing

- Selling things online for other people (on eBay or other auction sites)

- Sidewalk caricature drawing

- Tax preparation

- Tutoring

- Web site designing

- Wedding planning

- Window washing

- Yard work, including lawn mowing

If you've ever thought, "I could use somebody to do that for me," someone else has probably thought that, too. The best business ideas come when you and the people you know realize that something isn't being done, or isn't being done as well as it could be. That's your cue to fill in the gap, and make some money yourself!

If you are unemployed

The minute you find yourself unemployed with little or no financial backup, you need to find work. If you can find another job in your field right away—great. That doesn't always turn out, however. Through no fault of yours, your specialty may not be in demand. Maybe five years ago they were offering signing bonuses, extra vacation time, and pool tables in the break rooms to hire people like you, but today you might have to wait in line for a job. In other cases, the job that's perfect for you isn't open yet. It's even possible that you need to update your skills or consider something related to your field, but not exactly what you've been doing. In any case, you need to take action now.

A common mistake people make is to think, "I could use a break. Unemployment checks aren't so bad. I'll start looking seriously in a month or two." They start sleeping late, puttering in the garage, and sending out just enough résumés to qualify for unemployment bene-. fits. Before they know it, four months have gone by, and their unemployment benefits may be about to run out. Now's the time to panic!

I was working for a software company in the '90s when all 250 of us employees were called into a special meeting. The company was closing its local offices, and we were all being laid off. If we wanted our severance pay, we had to stick around another two months and finish a few ongoing projects. Naturally, people were angry. They didn't all respond the same, however. Some looked dazed or slightly ill and went straight home. Others gathered in cubicles to gripe and gossip. A few walked straight back to their desks and started looking at job postings on the Internet. They were as disappointed as the rest of us, but they didn't waste a moment complaining.

Over the next two months, as the Last Day approached, the differences between the motivated few and the rest of us became more apparent. We didn't have enough to do, so people organized online group card games. You could hear them whooping about their wins or losses over the tops of their cubicle dividers. Some people got so bored that they watched each other play Free Cell. The few go-getters, however, I never saw play a computer game, or even stop to chat for more than a few minutes. They typed résumés, made calls, and looked at Help Wanted ads all day. One by one they got jobs and left.

I suspect that the difference between the computer game players and the go-getters was that the go-getters took the situation more seriously. Most of them had a family that depended on them to bring home a paycheck. Nobody was going to pick up the slack for them. I wonder, though, how many of the rest waited too long to get back in the market and found themselves in financial trouble as a result.

I confess that I got pretty good at computer Scrabble before I decided what direction I wanted to go next. I took classes that summer to update my computer skills. I also worked temporarily in an accounting office until the perfect job opened up—one that used the skills I had learned in the company that closed down.

If weeks go by, you don't have a job, and you don't have a financial reserve, it's time to find something. Almost anything. It's normal to be afraid that you will get stuck in a temporary job. You could have ten years invested in, say, Web design. If you start delivering pizzas, will you get stuck doing that for the rest of your life? You can reassure yourself, however, that you are only stuck if you let yourself be. Keep your Web design skills sharp, even if that means doing volunteer work or small jobs, and keep looking for work in your field. Taking temporary work outside your field in the meantime can keep you going until you get the work you want.

Time and again I see people who have been laid off simply not work for months, or even years, while they wait for the right job to come along. Not only do they run through all their unemployment benefits and their money, but now they've got a big hole in their résumé to explain. It would be far better for them to get out of the house and do something—anything—to keep some money coming in and to stay active.

Keep your eyes on a permanent job while you work a temporary one

Your main objective is not only to make ends meet but also to get back into a permanent position. Look for a temporary job that can help you expand your skills and meet people who can give you leads or even hire you. It should also be a job that lets you keep looking for a permanent one. You can hold down a swing-shift or night-shift job and still be available for daytime interviews. Or, if you can be open with your new employer about the fact that you are looking for a permanent position, you may be able to take time off for interviews.

Jobs to avoid

This is not the time to try anything risky. You can't afford to make a big cash investment or take other big risks. Some jobs can cost you more than they pay.

For example, avoid jobs that could compromise your health, and be honest about your limitations. The thing you can least afford to lose is your health. No matter how well a job pays, for instance, don't say that you can lift heavy packages if you really shouldn't. Check out safety records and talk to people who've tried it before you sign up for, say, a fishing season in Alaska.

If you use your home or car for your own business or as an employee, make sure you have insurance that covers property damage and liability. For example, if you use your own car to deliver pizza without telling your insurance company, you may not be covered for damage to your car and to other drivers if you cause an accident. Most personal car insurance policies exclude coverage for business use. Check your insurance policy or call your insurance company before you take a job that requires you to use your own car. If you have a spotty driving record, you probably shouldn't deliver pizza anyway. The risk of having an accident is too high.

Don't compromise your ethics. Don't sell a product that you don't believe in, and don't have anything to do with questionable business practices. If you have a funny feeling about promoting something, ask yourself if you would sell this to your best friend. If not, forget it. It won't be worth it.

As always, be skeptical of anything that sounds too good to be true. People are especially vulnerable when they really need money, so be careful.

Step Three

Make the Best Use of Your Money

10 Get Organized

*Take control of
your money today*

Disorganization often goes hand in hand with money trouble. Sometimes trouble is the result of disorganization; other times it's a contributing cause. When a shortage of money causes bills to pile up, the last thing people want to do is look at their bills and organize their papers. Even if they are just a little disorganized or are on a tight budget, facing those stacks of bills and papers can be downright painful. Getting organized is worth the trouble, however. In fact, it's the first step you must take if you want to take control of your finances and get a fresh start.

Before we start organizing, just look at what we're up against. Giant piles of paper. Coupons, bills, ads, notices—and all that can come in one envelope! It's the mail carrier's fault: It would be easy to keep the countertops cleared off if she didn't bring an armload of this stuff every day. If you live with other people, multiply the mess by the number of people in your household. They all walk in the door and plop down stacks of flyers, homework, grocery lists, and phone messages. They rifle through the stacks you've started to sort, take the good magazines, and wander off. No wonder you can't get ahead!

A few simple, inexpensive strategies can help you win the battle. You don't need to make a major investment down at the office supply store to get organized, either. Most of these strategies can be used with things you already have on hand.

Make one designated place for bills

It's absolutely essential that you have one place—and *only* one place—for bills. Only bills go in the bill place. When bills come in the door, they go directly there. Do not set them on the countertop or put them by the phone to sort later. Never, ever, scoop them up with other papers and hide them in a back room because company is coming. (I've done that. Bad news!)

One of the quickest ways to damage your credit rating is to lose bills that should be paid. The smaller the bill, the easier it is to overlook. It's a shame to mess up your credit score over bills that you could have paid if you could have found them. No matter how difficult your financial situation is right now, you must be able to find all your bills so you can make the best use of your money. If you can't pay a bill, you may need to call and make other arrangements. Besides, it is very important that you at least review all your bills when they come and make sure they are correct. If you don't protest most bills within a certain number of days, your creditors will assume the bill is right.

So you want your bills to always go directly to the bill place. For this to happen, the bill place must be easy to get to. You should be able to use it one-handed. If you grab the mail on your way into the house, you probably find yourself standing there with coat, purse or briefcase, keys, and mail. You can't put the bills in a file folder in a cabinet in the back office while you're holding all that stuff, so what do you do? You set the mail down. Now it's mixed with yesterday's mail, and the phone is ringing, so you'll sort it later. To avoid that scenario, try to make putting the bills away a little easier. Before you set down the pile, pull out the bills. On any given day, you probably get three or four bills at the most. Take everything that looks like a bill and stick it in that bill place you have ready—one that is nearby and that you can put things into with one hand. I use a small plastic bills holder that sticks to the outside of my file cabinet. I don't even have to open the file drawer. You can use anything from an executive-style oak box to a shoe box; what matters is that you have that one special place for bills.

Only bills, including both bills you get in the mail and payment coupon books, go in the bill place. Ads, coupons, order forms, and sales you might want to go to are not bills, and they will quickly overwhelm your bills and make it easy for you to miss bills that need to be paid. Put all those nonbills in another file or box.

Everyone in your house must know about the bill place, and everyone must use it without fail. Don't let anyone come to you later and say, "Why didn't you pay this bill? It was right here by the toaster." You don't pay bills by the toaster. If they want you to pay a bill, they'd better put it in the bill place.

Designate one person as the bill payer

One person in your household should be responsible for paying the household bills. You can trade off occasionally (not a bad idea if somebody wonders, "What's so hard about paying bills?"), but one person should be in charge. Otherwise, some bills may get paid twice and others not at all, and two of you may call the phone company and complain about the same questionable bill. Some things, like paying bills or driving a car, must be done by one person at a time.

Make sure the other adults in your household understand the basics of your system. Even if you never get sick or need anyone to take over the job, they do need to know what's going on. Of course, they need to know how very, very important it is to put the bills in the right place, but they also need to know why you pay the bills when you do and how they can find the current balance and pending payments on the joint checking account. You can't blame them for messing up your system if they don't know what it is.

Set up a bill-paying station

Paying bills is much easier if you can set up a place with everything you need where you can work on your bills undisturbed. A desk is great, but even a small table will do. Have everything you need within arm's reach: envelopes, pens, checkbook, stamps, and your computer if you pay bills online. If you can reach your filing cabinet without getting up, so much the better. Don't forget a large wastebasket; the best way to keep a clean desk is to always have a wastebasket handy.

Establish a paper-handling routine

You have your bill place and your bill-paying station set up, and you've decided who is responsible for paying bills. Now you need a streamlined paper-handling routine to make your life easier.

Think of yourself standing by the door, holding a giant stack of mail again. You pull out everything that looks like a bill and put it straight into your bill place, the one nearby that you can use one-handed. Any checks go directly into your purse or wallet—we're not losing those. Next stop, garbage or recycling can. Most of what's left can probably be tossed without further ado. In fact, the more quickly you throw away advertisements, the less likely you will be tempted by things that you didn't need until you saw the ad. That's the way it works for me, anyway. I'm better off tossing the ads, the catalogs, and even most coupons sight unseen. I never miss them.

With your bills put away and all the ads and other trash tossed, you shouldn't have much left. Have a place for each person's private mail, and a coffee table or other place where you always keep new magazines. Immediately transfer information such as dentist appointment dates onto your calendar—before anyone can lose the reminder card.

Whatever else you regularly get in the mail, categorize it and decide where you will keep it. You might need another box for things other than bills that you need to show someone or deal with later. Just make sure everything doesn't get tossed in there. The less you keep, the more easily you can find the things you really need.

Handle it once!

Almost all the paper and other stuff that comes our way should be handled once—twice at the most. The more times you have to hold a piece of paper and figure out what to do with it, the harder the job of staying organized will seem.

Sign up for direct deposit

One thing you don't want to leave to chance is getting your checks to the bank. The fastest, most surefire way to get your money into your account is by direct deposit. With direct deposit, your check can't get lost in the mail or misplaced around the house. It gets deposited faster than you could get it and drive to the bank, you don't waste gas and time getting it there, and you still get a payment stub in the mail that shows your gross income and all your itemized deductions for the period. It's a great deal all around.

Most large and midsized employers now offer direct deposit. You can even get government checks, such as unemployment compensation and Social Security benefits, by direct deposit. Your employer or someone at the relevant government agency can tell you how to set it up; generally you just need to supply a voided original check or a photocopy so the paying bank can see the routing and account numbers at the bottom of your check.

Pay your bills

Chapter 11 explains how to prioritize your bills when you don't have enough money to pay them all in full. In this chapter, you'll learn good bill-paying habits that can help you stay organized, save time, and avoid problems.

Decide how often and when you will pay your bills

Twenty years ago, most bills were due in thirty days. You could pay your bills once a month and probably be fine. Nowadays, many creditors expect to be paid within twenty days of the day *they print your statement.* After you get the bill in the mail, you have about ten days to pay it and send it out again, more or less. Unless your bills all come at the same time every month, you probably need to pay them every week, or at least twice a month.

Decide what day you will pay your bills, and put it on your calendar. It can be the same day each week, or every payday. From now on, you pay bills that day. If you don't have enough money to pay them all, this will be the day that you go through your bills and deal with them. Dealing with your bills on a regular basis is too important to be left to chance.

Open and read every bill

You must review your bills when you receive them to make sure they are accurate. If you find a discrepancy or a charge you don't recognize, call the company immediately. Check for late fees, service charges, and changes in interest rate. Many people pay a higher interest rate on their credit cards than they think. They never noticed when the rate went up.

Immediately throw away all the extra junk that comes with your bills—the "free" offers with outrageous shipping and handling charges, the coupons, and all the other hitch-a-ride advertising that gets stuffed into your statement envelopes.

Use automatic payments or debit cards

One way to simplify bill paying is to have fewer bills to pay. You can set up many bills, such as car payments and utilities, to be paid directly from your account. You can use a debit card instead of credit cards to have payments taken directly from your checking account;

you pay as you go, so there's no bill to pay at the end of the month.

Be sure, however, that you have enough money to cover these withdrawals from your account. If you use a debit card, write every purchase amount in your check register and keep careful track of your balance. You may want to set up only small bills to be paid automatically if you typically keep only a modest balance in your account. If you get paid the same day every month, you can set up your mortgage and other important bills to be paid automatically the next day. That way, these bills are always first in line to be paid.

Good bill-paying habits

Whether you pay bills by hand or online, always write the date paid on the bill or payment coupon. If you are using paper checks, also write the check number. If you pay online, note the confirmation number. That way, if the payment is ever questioned, you have a record of when you paid, and you can find the canceled check or electronic payment.

You should also include your account number with every payment. It's not unheard of for payments to be credited to the wrong account. Make sure your account number is on the check or electronic payment to prevent misapplication of your payment, or to prove that you made your payment if it is lost.

Use your computer to pay bills

Paying bills used to mean writing checks by hand, copying the information into a check register, stuffing envelopes (and getting the address to show in the little window), adding your return address, sticking on a stamp, and taking the stack of bills to the mailbox. You could spend an entire evening paying bills.

Paying bills online speeds things up. The first time you pay each payee, you enter the address and other information online. From then on, you can just click on that payee's name and enter how much you want to pay and when. The bank's records show that you paid the bill, so if you ever need to, you can prove that you paid it. If you are tech savvy, paying your bills online is a good habit to get into, plus you save postage.

It's easy to pay bills ahead of time with online bill paying. If a bill is due sometime in the future, you used to have the choice of paying the bill early or putting it aside with the risk of forgetting to pay it when the time came. When you pay online, you tell the bank when you want the bill paid. You can look at your online account at any time and see the bills you have set up. The bank will even tell you the total of your pending bill payments, so you can make sure you have enough money in your account to cover them.

Paying bills online is not limited to paying large companies like the phone company and credit card company. You can pay anyone online, even someone like a babysitter or a music teacher. If the payee is not set up to be paid electronically, your bank simply issues a check and mails it to him.

Don't throw away all your paper checks too quickly, however. Depending on the payee and your bank, sometimes it takes longer to pay a bill online. Some banks may require up to eight days to process a payment and mail a check. If a bill is due right away, you may get the payment there faster by writing a check yourself and mailing or hand-delivering it.

Consider overdraft protection

If you have ever bounced a check—that is, had a check returned to the payee because you didn't have enough money in your account—you know how embarrassing that can be. It's also expensive. If you bounce a check that you wrote to a store, the store may charge you $25 or more for a bounced check fee. If it bounces again, the store can charge you again. Plus, the bank charges an additional fee. With overdraft protection, you can avoid embarrassment as well as bounced check fees.

Overdraft protection can be in the form of a temporary loan or of a link to another account you own, such as a savings, money market, or credit card account. Be careful that you don't start thinking of the overdraft buffer as part of your checking account; if you burn through that, you will once again find yourself bouncing checks. Also be aware that the bank may charge you fees and interest when you use overdraft protection.

Get rid of extra accounts

Most people have more credit card accounts than they need. It's no wonder—it seems that every store you go into wants you to open an account, and they all offer the most tempting discounts and rewards to get you to do it. To simplify your bill paying and improve your credit score, try to consolidate or pay off as many accounts as possible. An added incentive is that your minimum payment on one card will generally be less than your total minimum payments on two or more cards with the same overall total.

Don't just cut up the cards: The account will still be open. Write a letter to the bank requesting that it close the account. If you have a balance that you cannot immediately pay off, see if you can transfer it to a card you intend to keep. Watch out for transfer fees, though, and make sure it's worth it. In some cases, you may be better off paying down the debt where it is.

To cut down on paperwork, you might also want to consolidate some of your bank, brokerage, and retirement accounts. Having too many accounts not only creates extra paperwork but makes it more difficult to manage your investments well. You may even be paying more in maintenance fees than you would pay if you consolidated your accounts.

If you consolidate retirement accounts, be sure to use direct rollovers—that, is have the money sent directly to the other account, not to you—to avoid income tax repercussions. Ask your tax professional or a representative from the financial institution for more details.

Organize your files

To keep records and receipts organized, you need a filing system. A filing cabinet is great, or you can get a plastic or expandable filing box at the office supply store for not too much money. You can even use a cardboard box if you can find one that fits file folders. I like hanging files: They keep the folders from sliding around and under each other, and they make it easy to slip papers into the right folder.

If your finances are simple, you only need a few folders. You'll want one for receipts, one for medical records, and one for bank statements. Before you get your first tax document in the mail, make a folder for the most recent tax year. If you have a small business, you need a folder for that—or a separate filing system if the business has a lot of paperwork, such as for payroll. Look through your stacks of paper and try to categorize them. The more you can keep things in separate folders, the more easily you will be able to find records when you need them.

Even the best filing system becomes unworkable when it gets overloaded. Maintain your files by routinely throwing out things you no longer need and putting old papers in long-term storage. (Don't forget to shred sensitive papers, including any that show your Social Security number and date of birth.) You generally need old receipts and bills only for items that are tax related or that you may want to return or make a warranty claim on at some time. Every new year, put last year's receipts and bills in another folder or a large envelope where you can find them when you need to prepare your taxes. After tax season, clearly mark the folder or envelope and stash it away, leaving room in your file system for this year's papers.

Some papers are too important to keep in a file box in the spare room. Your original will, life insurance policies, marriage and birth certificates, and power of attorney are better kept in a fire-resistant safe deposit box in your home or at the bank. Be sure to tell your family where they can find these papers if they need them.

Nowadays, many of your records may be on your computer. Computers don't crash and lose everything as often as they did ten or fifteen years ago, so it's easy to get complacent about backing up data. However, hard drives still die, computers get stolen, and data even gets accidentally deleted. Back up your financial data onto floppy disks, CDs, or an online server, and keep backing it up regularly. There's still no substitute for paper records: The technology never gets out of date, and you can easily tell what a piece of paper is at a glance. It's a good idea to print out long-term records like bank statements if your bank no longer sends you a paper copy.

How long should you keep records?

The length of time you need to keep your records depends on what you might need them for. For example:

- About a month is long enough for minor purchases, credit card slips, and so on. Make sure your credit card slips agree with your statement, and compare your bank deposit and withdrawal receipts to your bank statement. Throw out cash receipts for small purchases not related to taxes after you record the expenditure on your budget.

- Three years is long enough to keep most household bills and receipts for medium-sized purchases. If it's something you'd want to return if it falls apart or quits working, save the receipt for the life of the item.

- Seven years is the minimum length of time you should keep check registers, bank statements, and receipts for tax-deductible expenses. The IRS can audit returns up to three years after the return is filed, or longer if they think you underreported income or failed to file a return.

- Keep receipts for home improvements and other major assets until seven years after you sell the related assets.

- Keep tax returns, annual retirement account statements, insurance policies, birth certificates, marriage certificates, car titles, and house deeds forever.

Going Forward

Once you have a place for everything and you get in the habit of dealing with mail and piles of paper the same way every time, life should be much less stressful. You know where everything is, and nothing vitally important is being forgotten under stacks of paper. You're ready for the next step: prioritizing your bills.

11 What to Pay First

You've got a stack of bills on one hand, and a paycheck or other money on the other. You've been looking forward to getting this money, thinking that at last you will be able to pay your bills. The sad truth, however, is that by the time the money gets there, you already have more bills than cash—at least if you want to buy groceries and gas this month. What do you do now?

It would be great if you could pay them all—in full. Sometime soon, you will be able to pay everything. This month, you're going to have to make some choices. In the real world, you have to choose what you pay depending on what happens if you don't pay. That's why, before you write the first check, you need to know what can happen to you if you don't pay each type of bill.

What happens if various types of bills are not paid

It's usually less scary finding out what will probably happen than it is not knowing. This chapter tells you briefly what happens if you don't pay the most common types of bills. Although this all seems rather unpleasant to read, remember that you are only using this information to determine where to allocate your limited amount of money right now. By taking the steps in this book, you will avoid the worst of the consequences described below as you improve your total financial picture.

Rent. If you don't pay your rent, you may get a call or a visit within a week. If you still don't pay, or if your landlord starts proceedings against you immediately, you may be evicted in weeks or months. The length of time you can stay in an apartment or rental house if you are behind in your rent depends on state law.

Mortgage. You can be a few days late on most mortgages without getting much of a reaction, but if you go beyond the grace period—fifteen days or so—you may get a hefty late fee. Your mortgage coupon or statement should show the due date as well as the last day you can pay without getting a late fee. It should also tell you what the late fee will be.

If you miss more than one mortgage payment, you are in danger of foreclosure proceedings—the legal steps the bank takes to take your house away from you so they can sell it and recoup what you owe. Foreclosure proceedings generally take at least three months, depending on state laws. If your house is foreclosed on, you lose your equity, your credit rating takes a severe hit, and you have no place to live. If the bank sells the house for less than you owe, you may still owe it the rest.

Car loans. Car loans are secured by the cars themselves. If you're a few days late, you might get a late fee. After a few weeks, you could get a phone call and some demanding notices in the mail. If you are very late, a tow truck can pull up to your home or workplace and take your car away. Because a car is not considered as essential for survival as a place to live, state laws are less protective of cars. You can lose your car much more quickly than you can be evicted from a house or apartment.

Utilities. If you don't pay your utilities, they eventually get turned off. Utilities used for heating are considered essential, however, so most state laws give you a little time. You don't want to let things get to the point where they're turned off, however. You may be able to get by without them for a bit and even figure that you're saving money, but it will probably cost you more than it saves. The utility company probably charges a fee to reconnect your services, and also may want a deposit from you. If you move away, your record of falling behind on utility bills may follow you and make it harder for you to get utilities in the next place.

Credit cards. Although credit card companies can't take away your house or your car just because your payment is late, they have two major ways to motivate you to pay: additional fees and negative information on your credit report. They may also freeze your account, so that when you're standing at the register in a store, usually with five people in line behind you, you'll discover that your card doesn't work anymore. They can also raise your interest rates without prior notice, based on your late payment history.

If you stop paying your credit card bills, it will be almost impossible for you to get credit, and the credit card companies will use the standard legal methods, from collection agencies to liens, to get paid. With interest rates and late fees, the bill can keep growing at an alarming rate.

Phone bills. If you don't pay your phone bill on time, you will get notices in the mail. If you still don't pay, your phone service will be cut off.

Medical bills. Medical bills are a bit different. The doctor can't take back his services, and the hospital may be required by law to serve you next time you get sick—even if you haven't paid your bill. That doesn't mean that they have no recourse, however. They can send you notices, refer your case to a collection agency, and, if enough time goes by, take more drastic action such as placing liens on your property. Also, a private physician or other professional is not generally required to see patients who don't pay, so you may have difficulty getting health care.

Student loans. The federal government guarantees many student loans, which helps you in some ways and makes it harder in others. If you can't make your payments and you talk to the lending institution about it, they are more likely than most creditors to work something out. If, however, you let it slide, the government can employ more aggressive tactics than a private collection agency—for example, taking your tax refund, a collection method that other creditors can only dream of.

Taxes. It generally takes longer for government agencies to notice and start sending serious letters about past-due payments than it does other creditors, but once they decide to collect they have some very practical ways to do it—including taking money directly from your checking account. Whether you owe income taxes, property taxes, or any other taxes, the penalties and interest can quickly surpass the original amount you owed.

Tuition. Most schools try to work with you if you are late on a tuition payment, but if you are too late, you or your child can be out of the program. This can be traumatic for children, of course. For older students, missing a quarter or a semester can delay graduation and the potentially higher earnings that should follow.

Child care. If you need child care to work, unless you can make other arrangements such as having a relative care for your children, this is an essential bill. The day-care center can refuse to take your children if the bill isn't paid. When you can't work, your money problems only get worse.

Insurance. When your rent is due, it's easy to see insurance bills as relatively nonessential. What are the chances of getting in a car accident or having the house burn down if you are uninsured for a few weeks? Insurance companies have a strong defense, however. If you are one day past the deadline, your insurance is no longer in force. If you do have a catastrophic accident, you can lose a great deal in one day. If you can't afford to pay for your insurance, you certainly can't afford to replace your car—and the car you ran into—without it. Also, if your insurance is canceled for nonpayment, you may have a hard time reinstating it.

If you don't pay the fire insurance on your home, your bank will receive a notice from the insurance company that your fire insurance is no longer in force. Since most mortgage contracts stipulate that the borrower must carry fire insurance on the property, the bank will consider your loan to be in default.

Cable and Internet fees, health club memberships, magazine subscriptions. If the service or purchase isn't essential, the bill isn't, either.

Personal loans. If you've borrowed money from your mom or your best friend, unless she went through the formal paperwork of getting a mortgage on your property or otherwise protecting her interests, you probably can put her off for a while. If she is counting on the money, or if you are ashamed to admit that you don't have it, this can be a hard thing to do. Most of us would rather withhold payment from the bank than from Mom.

General steps that creditors take

Almost any creditor, with the general exception of friends and relatives, will report you to the credit bureaus when you are thirty days or more late. Other collection tactics may include:

- Calling you on the phone

- Sending collection letters with escalating levels of urgency

- Going to small claims court

- Garnishment (taking part of your wages)

- Sending your account to a collection agency, which will spend more time trying to collect your money

- Repossessing property, such as a car or a refrigerator

- Getting a lien on your property, such as your house, so they will get paid when you try to sell your property

Don't get too discouraged by the list of bills and the consequences of not paying them. Remember that the sooner you start taking steps to prevent these consequences, the better your results will be. The rest of this book explains your options in more detail and talks more specifically about different types of bills. However, the first thing to do is to put your bills in order.

Sorting and prioritizing bills

Now that you know what will happen if you don't pay each type of bill, you can decide what gets paid now, what you'll pay later or pay only in part, and what can wait. Of course, your situation may be different and you may have different priorities, but in general you can group your bills something like this:

Priority 1: Pay now

- Rent or mortgage

- Utilities

- Car payments (if you use your car to get to work)

- Insurance (health, life, and auto)

- Child care (if you need child care so you can work)

Priority 2: Pay as much and as soon as possible

- Credit cards

- Phone bills

- Student loans

- Taxes

- Tuition

Priority 3: Pay last

- Medical bills

- Personal loans

- Cable and Internet fees, health club memberships, magazine subscriptions

Bear in mind that even with a Priority 1 or Priority 2 bill, you can take steps to reduce your cost or to negotiate a lower payment when you are in a financial crisis. For example, if you rent your home, making your rent payment is the highest priority. Chapter 13 discusses ways to negotiate a lower rent payment, trade rent for services, or find a cheaper place to live if your rent is more than you can afford.

Step-by-step instructions

You have your bills, and you've thought about which ones are the most important. That's the hard part. Now you can figure out exactly what you can pay right now. Follow these steps to make the best use of the cash you have available, using the Bills to Pay worksheet below. You can also download the Microsoft Office Excel worksheet from HelpICantPayMyBills.net. This exercise is much easier to accomplish on a computer spreadsheet because you can adjust the numbers as much as you want, and the totals will automatically change as well.

1. List your current bills and minimum payments due. Enter them under the Priority 1, 2, or 3 headings as appropriate, in both the Payment Due and the Amount to Pay Now columns.

Help! I Can't Pay My Bills

Bills to Pay

Date _____

Cash on Hand				
Cash Reserve				
Cash Available to Pay Bills				

	Bill or Creditor Name	Payment Due	Amount to Pay Now	Total by Priority	Grand Total
Priority 1					
1	Rent or mortgage				
2	Electricity/gas				
3	Water				
4	Car payment				
5	Insurance				
6	Child care				
7					
8					
	Total Priority 1 Bills				
Priority 2					
9	Credit card 1				
10	Credit card 2				
11	Credit card 3				
12	Phone bills				
13	Student loans				
14	Taxes				
15	Tuition				
16					
17					
18					
	Total Priority 2 Bills				
Priority 3					
19	Medical bills				
20	Personal loans				
21	Cable				
22					
23					
24					
25					
26					
27					
	Total Priority 3 Bills				
	Total Amount to Pay Now				
	Balance or shortfall				

Enter the total cash you have on hand (Cash on Hand) and the amount you need to save out for daily expenses until you get paid again (Cash Reserve). Using the List of Debts worksheet you created in Chapter 2 and your current stack of bills, enter the Priority 1, 2, and 3 bills you need to pay in the Payment Due column. Then enter amounts in the Amount to Pay Now column and make adjustments in that column until the Total Amount to Pay Now (at the bottom of the page) is no more than your Cash Available to Pay Bills.

2. Enter the total amount of money available until the next paycheck or other money comes in (Cash on Hand).

3. Enter a Cash Reserve—the amount of money you need to save out for groceries, gas, and other essentials.

4. Subtract the Cash Reserve from your Cash on Hand. This is the amount of Cash Available to Pay Bills.

5. Add the Amount to Pay Now column for each priority level, and then add the Total by Priority column. Enter the result in Total Amount to Pay Now.

6. If the Total Amount to Pay Now is less than your Cash Available to Pay Bills, go ahead and pay all the bills on your list. If not, proceed to step 7.

7. Adjust the Amount to Pay Now column until the Total Amount to Pay Now is equal to or less than your Cash Available to Pay Bills. See individual chapters in this book on communicating with creditors and dealing with specific types of bills. Don't just stop paying certain bills, even if they are Priority 3, without telling your creditors or trying to work out something with them.

Don't write postdated checks or bad checks

When you sit down to pay bills and you don't have enough money, it sounds easy to write a check and hope you can cover it by the time it reaches the bank. Don't do it. You can no longer count on several days' float for the check to get to the sender, to the sender's bank, and then to your bank. With computerized systems, everything works faster—at least when you don't want it to.

You should know that writing a check that's not covered by sufficient funds in the bank is a crime. If you write an occasional check that bounces (sent back to the sender unpaid, due to insufficient funds), you probably won't face consequences beyond bank fees and embarrassment. But if a prosecutor can show that you willfully write checks that you know will not be covered, you can be charged with a crime.

Some people even write checks from accounts that have been closed, or they put a stop payment on the check, telling the bank not to honor it when it comes in. Unless you place the stop payment order because of a genuine consumer dispute, you are committing a crime. Now, instead of just being late paying your bills, you have a crime on your record. You may have to pay hefty fines in addition to any insufficient funds fees imposed by the creditor and your bank, and you may have to go to trial or at least attend special classes for bad-check writers. You don't even want to start down this path.

If you're very sure that you have money coming in on a certain date, you may think you can write a postdated check. Again, this is not a good idea. The check you are expecting to receive may be late, or the creditor may forget to hold the check and may deposit it with all the others. Don't let collection agencies or anyone else talk you into postdating checks. You can pay bills when you get the money to do so, and no sooner.

12 Cut Back on Your Expenses

Plugging the holes in your wallet

Little things add up—and we're not just talking about lattes. Service charges, unnecessary insurance, ready-to-microwave food, knick-knacks, and whatnot can take away your money and give you little or nothing in return. Taking the time to find out where the money is going is absolutely essential. Suppose you have a hole, or lots of holes, in your wallet. Maybe your wallet is falling apart, but you can't afford a new one. Would you ignore the holes and let the money keep falling out until you can afford a new wallet?

By the time you finish this chapter, you should have found at least a few holes in your wallet and know how to fix them. You should have a budget and know how to stay on it. You may even start thinking about money and spending differently.

Deprivation is not the answer. Awareness of where the money goes is. To get the most from our money, we need a whole new way to look at it.

Changing the way we think about money

For financial success, think long term!

When I see advertisements that say how much something costs per day or week, I always assume that they're trying to make it sound like something costs less than it really does. Apparently they don't want you to think about what it costs per month—let alone per year. For the same reason, I'm suspicious when they tell me in large print what the latest porcelain collectible or miracle exercise machine costs per month, and I need a magnifying glass to find the total cost or how many months I'll have to pay. As people who manage their money well know, it's the long term that counts.

One of the marks of growing maturity in children is when they start thinking further ahead. A toddler runs on the emotion of the moment; I remember my daughter could laugh, cry, and laugh again seemingly in one breath. Later, you can see them thinking further ahead—to Christmas, to summer vacation. By age eighteen, they think way ahead and make big plans for their lives (at least we hope so!). It's exciting to watch them become more mature—the more so because we never know what plans they will come up with next!

The same holds true for people as they become more financially mature. You've probably met people who think only about getting through this month, if not this trip to the store. They don't stop to think about the long-term effects of money choices—everything is here and now. If the charge card still works so they can buy what they want, everything's OK. In their defense, they may think that there's no point in planning ahead; after all, they feel they have no choices to make as they struggle to survive day to day. They may even feel irritated by talk of long-term financial goals; it may sound like someone is telling them how to build a boat while they are drowning.

As people learn more about managing money and become more experienced financially, they start to take a longer view of things. They see how daily expenses add up each month, and then they start to think of how different choices affect them over the course of a year. As they take control of their money, they make plans that will give them more options over their lifetimes. It cannot be emphasized enough: The biggest difference between the novice money manager

Money Secret

Always think about what something costs you per month and per year. Don't be fooled by a low daily or weekly cost. It's the long-term cost that counts.

and the more savvy one is that the novice thinks primarily about getting by for the moment, while the savvy person thinks about the rest of the month, the year, and even his life.

Think about the trade-off for everything you buy

When you're trying to decide if something is worth what it costs, don't think only in terms of the dollar amount. Think about the other things that you could do with that money.

Some people see certain things as necessities, and when they see you spend money on something different instead, they think that is extravagant. I don't get cable TV. I've considered it over the years, but at $40 to $60 a month, I just don't think it's worth it for the few programs I'd have time to watch. Some people who think cable is a basic necessity would look askance at a cruise vacation, but a $60 deluxe monthly cable package for one year comes to $720—and you can choose from a number of cruises that cost less than that!

If you're deep in debt, you could probably get even more relaxation from paying down some debts than from going on a cruise. If you take the $60 a month and start paying down credit card bills, you will be in much better shape by the end of the year.

Get into the habit of always looking at various costs as trade-offs. If you buy this purse now because it's on sale, you won't be saving up for the boots you really wanted. If you go out to eat whenever you're too tired to cook, you won't have the money to go to a special restaurant for someone's birthday. If you buy a boat, you may have to work so hard for the payments and upkeep that you don't have time to enjoy it. If you spend almost everything you earn over a long period of time, you lose the option of retiring when you want to. Everything you buy is a trade-off for something else. Make sure the things you spend money on are worth it to you.

Keep your "lattes"

From what I read in personal finance articles and books, it seems like everyone wants to take away my lattes. They keep comparing everything from retirement contributions to debt reductions with the cost of daily lattes, the clear implication being that if we would only give up our lattes, everything would be fine. Maybe to them, a latte is an example of the ultimate waste of money—to which I say, "Nonsense!" To me, lattes are the mark of civilization. When I travel, I don't care if I'm in Timbuktu; if I find a Starbucks, I know I can survive.

For you, it may be something else. Maybe you need a pedicure now and then, or your cable sports channel. Or maybe you need an occasional babysitter so you can go somewhere—anywhere—and hear yourself think once in a while. Whatever is most important to you, try to find a way to keep it in your budget. You may have to cut back or find a cheaper version of it. If you're having a really tough time financially, you may even need to put it off for a while. But don't let anyone tell you that you should never have those little splurges that are important to you.

Splurge without breaking the budget

I wasn't even a coffee drinker until I worked at a company that had a subsidized Starbucks in the cafeteria. When my coworkers saw me drinking mint tea, they helpfully suggested that I try a mocha latte with whipped cream. Oh, my goodness. I could drink one of those every morning for my break! How about for my afternoon break, too? It also goes pretty well with breakfast. The only problem was that I could spend my month's food budget, not to mention my calorie allowance, on mocha lattes. The problem became worse if I bought lunch at the cafeteria every day. I could easily spend $12 a day, or about $264 a month, on my lunches and snacks. That's a serious bite out of my total monthly food budget!

I thought about kicking the latte habit, but I know myself: If I promise never to have another latte, the next time I have one, I'll be discouraged. I'll think I just don't have the willpower to stick to a budget, and I'll start drinking lattes every day again. So I tried to make a plan I could live with. I noticed that the third mocha latte of the day wasn't nearly as good as the first one, anyway. I needed to find a way to make mocha lattes special again.

For me, the answer to the latte problem was simple. At work, we used our cardkeys to prepay for food in the cafeteria. I decided how much I wanted to spend in the cafeteria each month, and I loaded that much onto my card on the first of the month. I figured that I could bring my lunch three days a week, buy the $1 drip coffee Monday through Thursday, and reward myself every Friday with one wonderful latte.

It worked. I kept my lattes, without spending hundreds of dollars a month on them. I didn't feel deprived, and I could still walk to the cafeteria with my coworkers to get my drip coffee the other four days a week. Of course, when I quit working there, I had to get my own latte machine. By then, I was spoiled. Fortunately, homemade lattes cost a fraction of the price of coffee shop drinks.

Avoid self-defeating ways of thinking

How you think about money makes a big difference in the choices you make, and in how much stress you feel as you make your decisions. All of us have learned old, self-defeating ways of thinking about money. It doesn't matter if we learned them from our parents or from TV and advertisements. See if you've ever had any of these thoughts:

- **"Everybody else gets to buy this."** Everybody doesn't buy it, and somehow they all get by. Many people who do buy this shouldn't. Besides, you're not everybody. You have to make decisions based on your current circumstances, not anyone else's.

- **"I deserve it."** Of course you deserve it. You've worked hard, and you're stressed out. Money doesn't care who deserves it, though. McDonald's ads notwithstanding, the real question is: "Do you deserve the even bigger stress you'll have after you spend the money?"

- **"I don't deserve it."** Maybe you've been told the opposite— that you aren't good enough for nice things, and that you'll never be one of the people who have money. That attitude is just as destructive because it keeps you from making a plan and believing you can do it. If you don't deserve to win, or if you believe that you will never be able to have nice things and financial security, why try?

- **"I'll buy it now and pay for it next month."** If you find yourself thinking this month after month, it's time to realize that, without a realistic plan, the next month you're hoping for, when you will have plenty of money to go around, almost never comes. Even if it does, isn't it a shame to have your money all spent before it gets here?

By starting to think about your finances in the long term and learning to take better control of your money, you can avoid these destructive thought patterns.

In chapter 3, you created a budget that showed what you are

currently spending. It's time to get out that budget and see how you can make a plan you can live with.

Your circumstances will dictate how severely you need to cut back. If you have a good income but your money has been slipping away, you may not need to make many changes. Simply making a comfortable budget with a nice margin for incidentals may be enough. If you are in a more difficult situation—for instance, if you are unemployed or if you are so far in debt that you don't see how you can get out—you may have to learn to live on far less, at least for now.

Example: Balancing Sam and Sandy's budget

Let's use Sam and Sandy's budget as an example. Sam works at a music store, and Sandy used to work as an administrative assistant. They were just getting by on their combined incomes when the company Sandy worked for closed down. Sandy has been home with the kids while she has been looking for work, and she is ambivalent about returning to work full-time. On the one hand, their son is doing so much better with more attention, and their daughter isn't catching as many colds now that she's not in day care. On the other hand, looking at their budget, they obviously can't live on one income with their current expense levels.

Here's where Sam and Sandy are right now:

As you can see on this worksheet, they have $2,400 coming in each month and $4,807 going out. That means they are $2,407 short every month. To survive, they are putting off some bills and piling other bills onto their already substantial credit cards. Something has to change—fast.

This budget worksheet divides expenses into two categories: fixed expenses and variable expenses. Fixed expenses are the ones that are the same every month, such as the rent, the car payment, and the cable bill. You can't change them without making big changes like moving or canceling services. Variable expenses give

Sam and Sandy's Budget   Date _____

Income	Current Monthly Amount	Goal Monthly Amount	Difference
Income	2,400		

Expense Category			
FIXED EXPENSES - Expenses that generally stay the same			
1 Cable and Internet service	60		
2 Car insurance	183		
3 Car payments	583		
4 Child care	0		
5 Credit card payments	350		
6 Health insurance	479		
7 Renter's insurance	80		
8 Income tax withheld from earnings	198		
9 Membership fees	0		
10 Other debt payments	100		
11 Other insurance	0		
12 Payroll taxes and other deductions from earnings	184		
13 Rent	800		
14 Tuition, education expenses	0		
VARIABLE EXPENSES - Expenses that vary from month to month			
15 Car maintenance	50		
16 Clothing	200		
17 Dining out	75		
18 Gas and oil (for car)	85		
19 Gifts	20		
20 Groceries	500		
21 Household repairs and maintenance	100		
22 Medical expenses not covered by insurance	50		
23 Miscellaneous	150		
24 Other transportation expenses (bus fare, taxi fare)	0		
25 Pet care	20		
26 Telephone bill	90		
27 Utilities	250		
28 Vacations, trips	200		
TOTAL EXPENSES	4,807		
INCOME MINUS EXPENSES	(2,407)		

you a little more leeway each month. You can cut back on groceries, turn the heat down, and put off weekend getaways if you have to.

Because you have more control over variable expenses in the short term, we'll start by looking at them.

None of these expense amounts is extravagant for a family of four. Yet they total $1,790—more than half of Sam's paycheck. Sam and Sandy sit down *together* (that part is important!) and decide what expenses they can pare down.

Variable Expenses

Expenses that vary from month to month	Current Monthly Amount
Car maintenance	50
Clothing	200
Dining out	75
Gas and oil (for car)	85
Gifts	20
Groceries	500
Household repairs and maintenance	100
Medical expenses not covered by insurance	50
Miscellaneous	150
Other transportation expenses (bus fare, taxi fare)	0
Pet care	20
Telephone bill	90
Utilities	250
Vacations, trips	200
Total variable expenses	1,790

At first they start slashing whole categories out. No dining out, no new clothing, no household maintenance. While that may be possible for one month, maybe two, that's not a realistic plan for long. That's like me trying to tell myself, "No more lattes—ever," and then not being able to stick to it! A budget must be livable or it will wind up in the trash.

Variable Expenses

Expenses that vary from month to month	Current Monthly Amount	Goal Monthly Amount
Car maintenance	50	50
Clothing	200	100
Dining out	75	50
Gas and oil (for car)	85	75
Gifts	20	10
Groceries	500	400
Household repairs and maintenance	100	25
Medical expenses not covered by insurance	50	50
Miscellaneous	150	50
Other transportation expenses (bus fare, taxi fare)	0	0
Pet care	20	20
Telephone bill	90	90
Utilities	250	200
Vacations, trips	200	20
Total variable expenses	1,790	1,140

Sam and Sandy find some places they can realistically cut back. They decide that they can stick to eating out once a month, in a nice but not too expensive restaurant, and cut their dining-out budget from $75 down to $50. Even though $200 is not a lot to spend on clothing for four people, two of whom are growing like crazy, they decide that with Sandy not going to an office, they can spend a bit less. If they really watch sales and if the kids wear more hand-me-downs from their cousins, they can cut the clothing budget back to $100 a month. Vacations might consist of driving to Grandma's house or going camping this year. The kids love camping anyway. Until they have a bigger budget, they can cut their vacation budget to $20 a month for extra gas money.

After going through their budget and trying to make a reasonable goal for each category of variable expense, this is what they come up with.

Now their variable expenses are $1,140—$650 less than they were. Sam and Sandy were running $2,407 short every month, however, so they need to find another $1,757. Next, they look at their fixed expenses to see what they can change. Here are their fixed expenses at their current level:

Their fixed expenses alone are $3,017—more than their monthly income of $2,400. Some serious work must be done to make this budget work!

Now that Sam and Sandy have made this budget, they understand better why they are having such a hard time. Without a budget, each often thought the other person was spending all the money—why else were they always so short of it? Now they can see that no amount of scrimping on cafeteria lunches and turning the heat down another degree is going to fix their money problem. They can stop fighting about where the money is going and together look for a solution.

For starters, Sam and Sandy decide to drop their cable and Internet service and save $60 a month. They live near the library, and they can check e-mail there. Without cable, they'll be going to the library more often to get books and videos anyway.

Fixed Expenses

Expenses that generally stay the same	Current Monthly Amount
Cable and Internet service	60
Car insurance	183
Car payments	583
Child care	0
Credit card payments	350
Health insurance	479
Renter's insurance	80
Income tax withheld from earnings	198
Membership fees	0
Other debt payments	100
Other insurance	0
Payroll taxes and other deductions from earnings	184
Rent	800
Tuition, education expenses	0
Total fixed expenses	3,017

They have a personal loan from Sandy's mom that they have been trying to pay $100 a month on. They get up the courage to ask her if they can postpone payments for the time being. She is more accommodating than they expected; in fact, she says that she doesn't need the payments right now and that they can postpone payments for as long as a couple of years. Sam and Sandy insisted on paying interest on the loan at about what Mom could make with a CD (certificate of deposit) at the bank. The interest will be postponed along with the payment. The three of them write a letter and sign it, so there won't be any misunderstandings about what they decided.

The payroll taxes and the mortgage are staying the same, as are medical insurance premiums and credit card payments. They file a new Form W-4 to reduce the amount of income tax they have withheld from Sam's paycheck (see chapter 7). They raise the deductible on their renter's insurance and save $30 a month.

The hardest decision that Sam and Sandy make is to part with one of their cars. They conclude that they can't make their budget work with two car payments and insurance on the two cars. Sandy protests that she doesn't want to be trapped at home without a car, but then she realizes that she can choose between being at home without a car and being at work just to pay for one. Besides, she can drive Sam to work on days when she needs the car. She talks to a couple of friends who get along with one car in the family, and suddenly it doesn't seem so impossible.

Sam and Sandy's new budget is vastly better—but not quite good enough. They can save $1,523, but they are still almost $1,000 a month short. Sandy was really starting to like the idea of staying home with the kids, at least for a couple of years, but now it seems out of reach.

Since they can't balance their budget solely by reducing expenses, they will to make more money, too. Sandy wonders if she can make money at home, without leaving the kids. She's seen a lot of ads for working at home, but on closer inspection she concludes that most of them are either outright scams or boil down to selling things to her friends and relatives. She considers going back to work and starts checking into various day-care options for the kids. Looking at the going rates for day care, she thinks, "I could make money doing that!"

Sandy's new business of providing day care doesn't take long to get started. She decides that she doesn't want to be tied down all day and that she really prefers working with potty-trained kids, so she advertises an after-school program for children ages three and up. She researches state licensing requirements and dives into her new enterprise with enthusiasm. She uses some of the money they got from selling her car to buy supplies and to make her house meet state safety requirements, she tells her friends and neighbors she's in business, and soon she has more business than she can handle. She doesn't make a ton of money, but it only takes a few hours a day, and she makes enough to cover their budget shortfall.

Sam and Sandy's new budget looks like this:

Sam and Sandy's Budget
Date _____

Income	Current Monthly Amount	Goal Monthly Amount	Difference
Income	2,400	3,300	900
Expense Category			
FIXED EXPENSES - Expenses that generally stay the same			
1 Cable and Internet service	60	0	(60)
2 Car insurance	183	133	(50)
3 Car payments	583	0	(583)
4 Child care	0	0	0
5 Credit card payments	350	350	0
6 Health insurance	479	470	(9)
7 Renter's insurance	80	50	(30)
8 Income tax withheld from earnings	198	157	(41)
9 Membership fees	0	0	0
10 Other debt payments	100	0	(100)
11 Other insurance	0	0	0
12 Payroll taxes and other deductions from earnings	184	184	0
13 Rent	800	800	0
14 Tuition, education expenses	0	0	0
VARIABLE EXPENSES - Expenses that vary from month to month			
15 Car maintenance	50	50	0
16 Clothing	200	100	(100)
17 Dining out	75	50	(25)
18 Gas and oil (for car)	85	75	(10)
19 Gifts	20	10	(10)
20 Groceries	500	400	(100)
21 Household repairs and maintenance	100	25	(75)
22 Medical expenses not covered by insurance	50	50	0
23 Miscellaneous	150	50	(100)
24 Other transportation expenses (bus fare, taxi fare)	0	0	0
25 Pet care	20	20	0
26 Telephone bill	90	90	0
27 Utilities	250	200	(50)
28 Vacations, trips	200	20	(180)
TOTAL EXPENSES	4,807	3,284	(1,523)
INCOME MINUS EXPENSES	(2,407)	16	2,423

Sam and Sandy learned to live on their new budget. Sam looked into ways to improve his job skills so he could make a better salary, and eventually they were able to add a few things back to their budget, including Internet service and loan payments to Mom.

Create a Goal Budget

You can do the same thing with your budget. Hopefully, your budget is closer to balancing than Sam and Sandy's was. Some people just need to cut their dining-out budget in half, switch to a basic cable package, and adjust their income tax withholding. Others, like Sam and Sandy, have to make harder decisions like selling a car, moving to a less expensive home, or putting off expensive vacations for the foreseeable future.

You already created a budget in chapter 3, showing your current income and spending amounts. Your current budget is very important; without it, making a new budget is mostly guessing. Now you can take your current budget and fill in the column for Goal Monthly Amount column. You can keep changing amounts until your income is greater than your total expenses. This is much easier if you use a spreadsheet program, so you don't have to keep adding and subtracting numbers yourself. You can find this Budget worksheet online at HelpICantPayMyBills.net, or you can use the one on the next page:

Line-by-line instructions for budget items

Go through each line in your budget looking for ways to cut expenses. The following suggestions may help you reach your goal of creating a budget with expenses that do not exceed your income. Each expense category below matches the line numbers on the budget worksheet.

Budget

Date _____

Income	Current Monthly Amount	Goal Monthly Amount	Difference
Income (enter gross pay before taxes and withholding)			
Expense Category			
FIXED EXPENSES - Expenses that generally stay the same			
1 Cable and Internet service			
2 Car insurance			
3 Car payments			
4 Child care			
5 Credit card payments			
6 Health insurance			
7 Homeowner's or renter's insurance			
8 Income tax withheld from earnings			
9 Membership fees			
10 Other debt payments			
11 Other insurance			
12 Payroll taxes and other deductions from earnings			
13 Rent or mortgage payment			
14 Tuition, education expenses			
15 Other fixed expenses			
VARIABLE EXPENSES - Expenses that are vary from month to month			
16 Car maintenance			
17 Clothing			
18 Dining out			
19 Gas and oil (for car)			
20 Gifts			
21 Groceries			
22 Household repairs and maintenance			
23 Medical expenses not covered by insurance			
24 Miscellaneous			
25 Other transportation expenses (bus fare, taxi fare)			
26 Pet care			
27 Telephone bill			
28 Utilities			
29 Vacations, trips			
TOTAL EXPENSES			
INCOME MINUS EXPENSES			

1. Cable and Internet service

Cable TV is an optional service. For me, it's not worth it. I've never had cable TV in my life, and I figure that over the last twenty years I've saved enough by not having cable to buy a small car. Remember the latte principle, though. If cable TV is top priority for you, try to cut other things first. If you can't afford cable for a time, motivate yourself to get control of your finances by promising yourself that you'll get cable as soon as you reach certain financial goals.

Internet service is also generally optional unless you need it for your business. It's still not true that everyone has it at home, and you can usually access the Internet at the library, or at work if your employer allows it.

2. Car insurance

Car insurance rates vary widely from company to company. Periodically compare insurance rates at other companies, but don't switch too often. You'll get better service if you stick around once you find a good company with competitive rates. Even if you stay with one company, you can take steps to lower your rates. For example:

- Before you buy a car, ask your insurance company how much it will cost to insure. Insurance rates vary because some cars are safer or cost less to fix when they are damaged. More expensive cars also cost more to insure because more value is at risk.

- Find out which safety and antitheft equipment your company will give you a discount for having installed on your car. Make sure you are getting credit for all safety and antitheft equipment you already have. Also find out if your insurance company gives a discount if you take a defensive driving course.

- If you have a kid who drives, make sure he or she knows about the good student discount. Assign him the least expensive car, and tell the insurance company that he primarily drives it. Also tell the insurance company when he is away at college without a car.

- Try to keep a clean record. Traffic tickets and accidents really do drive up your insurance rates—rapidly.

- Raise your deductible. Your rates can go down significantly when you bear more of the risk. When your car gets older, cancel collision insurance (the portion of your insurance that covers damage to your car) entirely; it's generally not worth the expense on a low-value car.

3. Car payments

Most people in financial difficulty have bought more car than they can afford (see chapter 17). If your car payments are more than you can handle comfortably, consider selling your car and getting one that you can buy with cash or with lower payments. If you have two cars in your family, you might be able to get by with one. If you live somewhere with public transportation, you can probably get by without a car, at least temporarily. Many people do.

Another way to lower your car payments is to see if you can get a lower-interest loan, such as a home equity loan or line of credit, to pay off your higher-interest car loan.

4. Child care

Child care is one area where you don't want to scrimp at your children's expense. However, child care can be a major expense, and more expensive child care is not necessarily better. Some preschools have become way overpriced by convincing parents that they give toddlers a better scholastic start. It's up to you to determine whether they really deliver, or if those French lessons are absolutely essential.

Some workplaces offer free or discounted child care. If the child care is provided near your workplace, you can save transportation costs and possibly see your child during breaks, too.

If you have relatives who can provide child care, they may be willing to do it for less (or possibly for free, if it's Grandma). It's hard to beat a one-on-one relationship with someone who loves your kids and will read stacks of books to them.

If you receive public assistance or have below-average income, you may qualify for reduced child-care rates in some areas, or the state may even help pay for child care while you work. Even relatives, including Grandma, can get paid by the state in some cases.

Another option is to stagger your work schedule with the other parent to cut down on or eliminate child-care expenses. Or, if you work part-time, you may be able to trade child care with someone who works an alternate schedule. Some employers are especially accommodating about arranging alternating shifts for you and your spouse if you both work for the same company.

5. Credit card payments

Your primary goal with credit card debt is to pay off or transfer from the cards with the highest interest rates. These are the debts that are costing you the most. If you have two cards with the same interest rate, try to pay off the smaller one or transfer it to the other; your minimum payment is generally lower on one card than on two with a comparable total balance.

You may also be able to lower credit card payments by requesting a lower interest rate. (Yes, you can just call and ask!) This has a better chance of success if you have been making your payments faithfully.

You may want to consider getting a home equity loan or other loan to pay off your debts so you only have one payment to make. Be careful, though, not to spend too much on refinancing charges and fees that set you back farther than ever. Avoid loan consolidation companies that make big promises and take big bucks from you. You can get loans from reputable banks and financial institutions. You don't need to work with businesses that advertise on power poles.

Credit card debt is discussed in more detail in chapter 18.

6. Health insurance

Health insurance is another area where you don't want to scrimp or quit paying and jeopardize access to the health care your family needs. However, most health insurance plans let you choose from

Deductible

An insurance deductible is the amount you have to pay in qualified expenses before the insurance company starts paying. A deductible amount may apply to each individual or to your entire family. Your deductible total generally starts over each calendar year.

different levels of deductibles and coverage for different costs. By raising your deductible amount or agreeing to see doctors within a network, you can usually save on insurance premiums.

You might also qualify for government help. For example, Washington state sponsors a health insurance plan called the Basic Health Plan for low-income residents who aren't eligible for Medicare and who meet certain other criteria.

Make sure that you are not paying for health insurance twice. For example, if you and your spouse both work and are having insurance premiums deducted from your pay, make sure you're not paying for overlapping insurance coverage. It won't do you any good to be twice-insured when you get sick; no insurance company will pay for something you've already been reimbursed for.

7. Homeowner's or renter's insurance

Don't try to save money by letting homeowner's or renter's insurance lapse. You could lose everything you own and then some. In fact, your mortgage may be in default if you let your fire insurance lapse. You can, however, save money by shopping around for rates at different companies. Every couple of years, compare prices again to make sure your rates are still competitive.

Look through your policy carefully and make sure everything is correct. For example, the premiums are less if you are closer to a fire station or to an authorized fire hydrant or water source, so make sure these facts on your policy are correct.

As with other types of insurance, you can save money on premiums by raising your deductible.

8. Income tax withheld from earnings

Most Americans have too much income tax withheld from their pay. One of the first things you should do to take control of your own money is to make sure you are having the correct amount withheld from your paycheck, which you can do by using the IRS Withholding Calculator on the IRS Web site at http://www.irs.gov/individuals. You can learn more about adjusting your income tax withholding in chapter 7.

9. Membership fees

Health clubs, the YMCA, professional clubs, and other places can be important to us and our families—or they can be something that sounded good when we signed up for them. If you have memberships that you are not using, by all means try to cancel them.

Clubs and other places often allow cancellations for hardship reasons such as illness, moving, unemployment, or divorce, even if no exceptions are mentioned in your contract. Or they may allow a suspension of your membership for a period of months. Most state laws require health clubs to let members freeze their memberships if they are temporarily disabled or to cancel their contracts if they become permanently disabled or die.

If you do use your memberships, you have to decide if you can afford to continue or, assuming you can get out of monthly payments, if you can do without until your situation improves.

10. Other debt payments

If you have other bank loans or loans from financial institutions, make sure that you are getting the best interest rate possible. If you are in an emergency situation, ask if you can pay only interest for a time, or postpone payments temporarily with a plan to catch up later. For more information on dealing with loans from financial institutions, see chapters 18 and 19.

If you owe someone such as your parents or friends, be honest with them and ask if they can take lower payments for a time. If they do agree to lower payments, make the payments faithfully, or they will be sorry they tried to help. Always get any change to a loan agreement in writing. Even just a letter from you to them, clarifying your new agreement, can save a lot of future misunderstandings.

11. Other insurance

If you have other insurance premiums, such as umbrella liability, disability, or business insurance, make sure that you actually need everything you are paying for and that you are getting credit for anything that should reduce your rate. Compare rates periodically.

If you have dependents, don't drop your life insurance. Make sure that you are not paying for more life insurance than you need, however, and consider switching to term insurance to get more for your dollar.

12. Payroll taxes and other deductions from earnings

You can't do much about Social Security and Medicare deductions from your pay, but you can check on your other deductions and make sure you're not paying for more than you need. For example, some companies take deductions for health club dues and political action groups, among other things. If you belong to a labor union, fees for other items in addition to your minimum dues may be deducted. Make sure you understand every item that comes out of your paycheck. If in doubt, ask someone in the payroll department. Don't let the Payroll Lady give you the brush-off; it's your money.

13. Rent or mortgage payment

Unless you move, your rent or mortgage payment is a fixed expense—and a top priority one at that. If you are having a temporary crisis, however, you may be able to get a reprieve. If your situation is more permanent, you may need to consider moving. It's better to live in a smaller house with less stress than to live in a bigger one and be constantly stressed about money.

For more information about rent, see chapter 13. For help with mortgage-related problems, see chapter 19.

14. Tuition, education expenses

Tuition and other education expenses are investments in yourself and the other members of your family. They can be one of the best investments you can make for a better future. Not all education expenses give the same rate of return, however. Ten or twenty years from now, what you learned will probably be more important than the status of the place where you learned it. You can do a lot to reduce your education expenses without sacrificing your dreams.

For elementary and secondary students, private schools can provide an excellent education. They can also be prohibitively expensive. You may be able to find a quality public school, or it may be cheaper to move to an area with good public schools than it is to live in an area where you feel the need to pay for private schools. You can also compare private school tuition rates. Some religious schools, for example, are subsidized by the denominations that sponsor them, and they may offer financial help if you need it. Another option that is becoming more popular in recent years is to teach your kids yourself. Some couples discover that it's cheaper for one parent to stay home and teach the kids than it is for both parents to work and pay private school tuition. Teacher-parents often do an outstanding job, too.

For college students, the costs of different schools vary even more widely. Some colleges cost more per year than the average person makes. Community colleges are still a bargain, and the student can save more money by living at home. Compare the prices at universities, including those in other parts of the country and in other countries if you are so inclined, before you settle on one. (Make sure the credits are transferable; check with the designated registrar of the school.)

On the other hand, if you or your child wants to try for an Ivy League school, don't be discouraged by the price tag. Some of the most prestigious schools offer the best scholarships.

The cost of college has risen faster than inflation over the last few years, but so has the number of programs to help students pay for it. You don't need to pay any scholarship search services. Check out http://www.fastweb.com/cpt on the Internet for help finding scholarships. Every institution of higher education also has locally funded scholarships. You should personally contact the financial aid offices of the colleges the student is interested in to find out about every potential source of help.

15. Car maintenance

Putting off essential car maintenance is not a long-term cost-saving strategy, and when you're strapped financially, it seems like you can count on your car needing work. Cars keep getting more complicated and computerized, so it's harder now than it was twenty years ago to do the work yourself or to ask Cousin Andy to look at it for you. You can still find ways to save money on car repairs and maintenance, however.

Many community colleges with automotive programs look for cars that need certain types of repair for their students to practice on. If the students are well supervised, you should be able to trust them to do a good job.

Be sure that you have a mechanic you can trust and return to whenever you need work done. Ask your friends for referrals. The most expensive maintenance mistake you can make is to use a mechanic who sees your car as a source of endless income. The good mechanics are priceless; treat them right and they will save you a lot of money over the long haul.

Try to buy a car that costs less to maintain. Some European or performance cars can cost twice as much to repair as the average car. Ask your mechanic which cars cost more to repair and which ones are likely to need more maintenance. Before you find a car, ask your mechanic to take a look at it; he can usually tell if a car will be spending more time in his garage than in yours.

If your car has a warranty, you don't necessarily have to go to the dealer for maintenance. Dealers often charge more than other repair shops. They tend to encourage the idea that you have to use them or your warranty may be void, but that's not usually the case. Read your warranty agreement to be sure.

Don't be unduly alarmed when the service light on your dashboard goes on. Ask your mechanic; sometimes the light is activated by mileage alone, and your mechanic can just turn it off for you.

16. Clothing

Some budget for clothing is a necessity. If you try to make a strict budget and say, "No new clothes," sure enough the strap will break on your favorite shoes, the kids will have a growth spurt, and the new spring styles will make the clothes in your closet look, well, old. You can't stop buying clothes altogether. You can stretch your clothing budget, though.

When I was growing up, a person could save a lot of money by sewing her own clothes. Nowadays, the price of fabric and a pattern often exceeds what you could pay to buy something already made. Sewing is a great creative outlet, and if you are a careful shopper it can still save you money, but it is not always such a great use of your time to sew all the family's clothes anymore.

Altering and mending clothes, however, can still save a considerable amount of money. If you buy kids' pants a little long and turn up a hem, for example, you can make them last two or three times as long.

If you want to stretch your clothing dollar, it pays to look in some different places than you are used to. It used to be easy to tell whether you had bought clothing at a discount store or at a nice department store. Now it's getting harder all the time, and if you learn how to look for nice fabrics and good sewing (the collar usually gives it away), you can find quality clothes in some surprising places. If you like designer labels, you can find them at overstock stores such as Ross Dress for Less. You have to look a little longer and try to get there when they've just received new shipments, but when you find clothes for 75% or so off department store prices, it can start to get fun.

To get really big savings, try buying used clothing. Not all of the clothing at Goodwill is even used, and some of it has been used very little. Used children's clothing is an especially good deal, and it's a popular item at garage sales.

Sample sales are another way to get clothing at less than department store prices. Salespeople travel with samples of clothing, and certain stores buy the samples and sell them. Some of them only carry merchandise at certain times; others keep regular hours.

If you have nothing to spend on clothes but you need some for your kids or to make yourself presentable for job interviews, try local churches and charities. Many organizations that have food banks also have clothing supplies to give away. They sometimes have drives in the fall to collect winter coats and give them to children and adults. Other organizations, such as Wardrobe for Opportunity (http://www.wardrobe.org) and Dress for Success (http://www .dressforsuccess.org), specialize in giving career clothing to low-income women. There's no reason for you or your children to go without the clothing you need.

17. Dining out

Dining out can be a relaxing social event, a break from cooking, and a treat for everyone. It can also be an overused fallback plan in which you pay too much for mediocre food and spend more time waiting for it to come than it would have taken to make it yourself.

It's so easy to fall into the habit of eating out too often. For one thing, it doesn't seem that expensive to grab a sandwich at the drive-up window. You can get a sandwich and a drink for, say, $5—how can that hurt your monthly budget?

If you grab that $5 sandwich once a month, it won't change your money situation much, but think about the long-term consequences if you do that day after day. For example, say you have two people in your household and you plan to spend $300 per month on food. If you each buy a $5 sandwich for lunch, that's $10, and you just spent your entire food budget on lunch ($10×30 days=$300). There's nothing left for breakfast, supper, or even bedtime snacks.

Another way to look at it is to compare the cost of making the sandwich to the cost of buying it. Say the bread is 20 cents for two slices, the cheese is 30 cents an ounce, and the deli beef is $1 for two ounces. Add another 10 cents for mayonnaise and pickles, and you have a $1.60 sandwich. Diet soda from a large bottle costs about 40 cents a pint. That brings you to a total of $2 worth of food, for which you just paid $5. So you paid $3 for the convenience of having someone make your sandwich. How long does it take you to earn $3? If you do that every day, $3 times 30 days is $90. Is that really what you want to spend $90 on?

Remember, it's your money, and no one can tell you how you should spend it. There are times when eating out is worth every penny. All too often, however, we pay too much for really substandard fast food, not realizing how it adds up over the course of the month and year.

18. Gas and oil (for car)

The U.S. Department of Energy recommends four ways to improve your gas mileage: driving more efficiently; keeping your car in shape; planning and combining trips; and choosing a more efficient vehicle. Depending on where you live, you might also want to become familiar with the mass transit system or ride your bicycle.

To drive more efficiently, take it easy on the gas and brakes. There's no need to keep stepping on it right up until it's time to brake for a light. At a price of $3.07 per gallon, each 5 mph you drive over 60 mph costs you an additional $0.21 per gallon for gas. Don't haul heavy things in your trunk unnecessarily. Use cruise control on the highways to help you maintain an even speed.

To keep your car in shape, make sure you get regular tune-ups. Serious engine problems can cost you up to 40% more in gas consumption, but even driving your car slightly out of tune costs you money in gas. Have your air filter changed regularly, and use the right grade of oil for your car. Check the air in your tires; underinflated tires cost you gas mileage, too.

Telecommuting, staggering work hours to avoid rush hour traffic, and carpooling are all good ways to reduce gas usage by planning ahead. One method of saving commuting expense and time that has become more popular recently is to work four ten-hour days instead of five eight-hour days. Combine errands when you can.

The cheapest car to drive is usually the one you have already, especially if you live in a state that charges sales tax on cars. Don't rush out and spend thousands of dollars on a different car to save a few hundred dollars a year on gas. If you are buying a car, however, go to the U.S. Department of Energy Web site at http://www.fueleconomy.gov/feg/findacar.htm and compare the fuel efficiency of different vehicles.

19. Gifts

Gift-giving can take on a life of its own. I have a friend who is in a circle of friends that celebrates everyone's birthday every single year. They also celebrate every holiday, and every celebration means gifts and more gifts. Most of the friends are dual-profession couples, and they seem to be able to afford a steady stream of very nice gifts. My friend can't afford to keep up with all this celebrating!

Fortunately, my friend has a knack for baking. Instead of buying expensive gifts, she bakes cookies and other goodies as only she can, and she gives them as presents. Everyone loves her cooking, and she never has to wonder if the gifts she gives will just gather dust!

Other people have different talents. Another friend was overwhelmed by the number of birthday parties her daughter was invited to, so she started making handmade doll clothes as presents. She found out if the birthday girl was into American Girl dolls or Barbie dolls, and she made outfits that were the hit of the party. One mother even called and asked if she could borrow the patterns—but the clothes had been made without any.

Gifts can be important to people. Gifts help make people feel special, and most of us feel like we're celebrating when we give and receive gifts. But gifts don't have to be extravagant. You can give a gift of your time, of something you make, or of something you already own that is meaningful. One of my favorite gifts is a teacup set that I received from my mother-in-law. She had owned it for years. My daughter has been admiring it, so one day it will be a gift to her. That's the kind of gift that people remember and appreciate.

20. Groceries

Many people shortchange themselves when it comes to food. They go to the grocery store and pay too much for low-quality food, just because it is convenient and packaged attractively. Most of the prepackaged foods in the stores, as a matter of fact, are cheaply produced and packaged in such a way that they can be shipped and stored almost indefinitely. They are so far removed from the farm or the orchard as to be almost unrecognizable. We can do better than that!

Take TV dinners, for example. The diet ones are the worst—they charge more for the privilege of selling smaller servings. Let's say you're in the mood for enchiladas. If you made enchiladas yourself, you would use fresh onions and peppers and big chunks of freshly cooked chicken. You buy a frozen diet enchilada, and if you're lucky enough to find a piece of pepper, you can drape it across your fork and it will hang there like a piece of cooked spaghetti. That poor pepper has had a long, hard journey from his home in the pepper field.

Store-bought cookies are another example. Mostly sugar and flour, cookies cost pennies to make. Yet grocery stores stock hundreds of kinds of ready-made cookies that cost up to $8 a pound, none of which can match the smell and taste of hot homemade snickerdoodles coming out of the oven. Why do we settle for less than the best, and pay so much for it?

Ironically, the quickest way to start saving money on groceries is to demand higher-quality food. Buy fresher food closer to its natural state, and you'll save money and eat like a king. You'll be healthier, too. Make an adventure of searching out farmer's markets in the summer, or grow your own vegetables. Head straight for the perimeter of the store, where the real food like produce, milk, and fresh meat is kept, and avoid whole aisles full of colorful packaging with very little food value inside. As a bonus, you'll find that it's actually more convenient to keep baking staples on hand than it is to buy mixes for each thing you might want to make.

Some other ways to save money on groceries:

- Buy in larger quantities when you have enough room and the food will keep.

- Buy in smaller quantities when you only need a little. For example, when I buy loose fresh ginger, I find a little nubbin that costs about 10 cents. Why buy more and throw most of it away?

- Always look at the price per pound or per item when you are comparing products. Generally, the smaller the package, the more the food costs per pound. After all, you're paying for all that packaging. Individual lunch packs are the worst!

- Don't pay for things you don't need. For example, resealable plastic bags for leftovers cost almost 10 cents apiece, while the old-fashioned kind with a twisty wire are about 3 cents each. Why use the 10-cent bag for jobs the 3-cent bag can do? Have you ever seen people put 7 cents' worth of leftovers into a 10-cent bag—and then throw it all out days later?

- Check out the sales and coupons, but don't get carried away. Sales and coupons only save you money if you needed the things anyway. Otherwise they *cost* you money.

- Make a grocery list and stick to it. Better yet, make a grocery list of things that you need to go along with food you already have on hand.

- If you are tempted by all that prepackaged food when you get to the store, try shopping online. If you live in an area that offers grocery delivery, you can avoid temptation by making your list online. You usually get fresher food because it comes directly from the warehouse, and the amount you save on gas and junk food should offset the cost of delivery.

- Learn to be a really good cook, not necessarily a fancy cook or a gourmet cook (whatever that is). Learn to prepare simple, fresh foods, and start paying attention to and appreciating all the wonderful food that is available.

21. Household repairs and maintenance

I used to think, when I lived in an old house, that the solution to constant home maintenance expenses would be to buy a new home. Then I got a newer home, and I found that it costs just as much to maintain. Unless you live in a rented place with a very attentive landlord, household repairs and maintenance are a fact of life.

Learning to do basic repairs and maintenance yourself can save a lot of money. For many repairs, the cost of supplies is nothing compared to the bill you will get if you pay someone to come out and do it for you. Be sure to get expert advice first, however. Buying the wrong supplies or installing them incorrectly can be an expensive mistake. You can usually get plenty of free expert advice at your local do-it-yourself center.

Some home maintenance can slide for a while when you are short of money. Other things, like leaky pipes, will cost you much more if they aren't fixed immediately. Ask someone knowledgeable what you can put off and what you shouldn't. You can sometimes find expert advice on the Internet. For example, at Ask the Builder (http://www.askthebuilder.com) you can e-mail Tim Carter specific questions and he will answer you.

When you do need a handyman or a contractor, hire someone who is qualified. Not everyone who claims to be a handyman knows what he is doing. Hire someone who is licensed and bonded, and for big jobs, don't sign the contract until you've gotten at least two estimates.

22. Medical expenses not covered by insurance

Medical expenses are hard to budget, because who knows when someone in the family will get sick or have an accident? Still, some families manage to spend less on medical care than others, without compromising their health by doing so.

First, become more knowledgeable about general health and preventive measures you can take to stay healthy. The best way to save money on health care is to not need it. Invest in your family's health by serving fresh, whole foods. Encourage them to spend more time outside, and make sure everyone has a chance to get enough sleep.

Find good medical and pharmacy providers and stick to them. A new doctor doesn't know your history. He doesn't know if a symptom is unusual for you or if you are a basket case. If you have to describe a long medical history to him, you will likely be charged for a full-length visit, and he still won't know as much about your case as if he had worked with you all along.

A good pharmacist can be a huge help as well. Pharmacists know a great deal about health and about prescription and nonprescription medicines. My pharmacist has saved me many trips to the doctor about minor ailments. He knows the best medicine for a cold sore that's starting up, and how to use it correctly. He always tells me what kind of cold or cough medicine I need. (I can never remember which is for "full" ears and which is for congestion.) He's a gem.

Don't expect pills to solve everything. Doctors prescribe pills so often because that's what their patients demand. Many patients don't think they've gotten their money's worth from an office visit unless they come away with a prescription—even if other measures would be more effective. For example, replacing wall-to-wall carpeting with hard floors and keeping the cat out of the bedrooms may help a child's allergies more than any pills can. Ask your doctor what you should do instead of, or in addition to, buying more prescription medicine.

If you do need a prescription, ask your doctor if she has prescription samples—especially if you haven't tried this kind of pill before and you don't know how it will set with you. Many people have expensive prescriptions going to waste in their cupboards because they found out they couldn't tolerate them. Take samples first. That's what they're for.

Many employers and other organizations offer free health hotlines that you can call with questions. When the baby is sick and you can't decide whether to go to urgent care or not, you can describe your symptoms to a health professional on the phone and get advice. You can also get help with nagging questions about your general health, or find out how often you should get checkups.

Avoid quackery. Don't fall for any special, secret, ancient, or any other kind of cure that sounds too good to be true. If the ad says that the medical establishment is conspiring to hide this miracle cure from you, forget it. That's ridiculous. Quackery is dangerous to your health and your wallet. The Arthritis Foundation estimates that for every $1 spent on arthritis research, $25 is spent on quack "cures."

That's money that could be better spent, and the cruelest blow is the false hope these scams give the people who can least afford to spend money and have their hopes dashed yet again.

23. Miscellaneous

Miscellaneous expenses can hit you from nowhere. They often seem small, but they add up over time. Larger miscellaneous expenses can derail the best budgets. The best you can do with miscellaneous expenses is to try to keep better track of them and then use your history of spending to plan more realistically for future months.

24. Other transportation expenses (bus fare, taxi fare)

If you take the bus, ferry, or vanpool to work, you should already be saving money on transportation costs. Find out if your employer subsidizes mass transit; many employers now cover the cost of a monthly bus pass.

25. Pet care

Sometimes pets can be more expensive than kids. Not all pet expenses are essential, however. A generation ago, most people groomed their own dogs and cats. Pets don't need expensive toys—like toddlers, they probably prefer the box it came in anyway. Many of the treats we buy for our pets are really for ourselves. Pets don't need them. A dog would rather sleep on an old coat that smells like you than on the most expensive dog bed.

Pet food costs can really add up. Some of the cheapest pet food is truly bad and can make Fido sick, but that doesn't mean that the top-of-the-line food is always worth the money. Something in the middle is probably a better bet. Some people stretch dog food with cheaper fillers like white rice; others successfully put their dogs on homemade vegetarian food altogether. Its important to make sure your pet gets complete nutrition. Ask your veterinarian or other pet-care expert how you can get the best pet food for your money.

26. Telephone bill

Unless you are a real estate salesperson or are in some other line of work that requires you to carry a cell phone, it's an optional service. We all got along without cell phones not so long ago, and many people still do. If you want to carry one for emergencies only, you can find cell phones that are tailored for that purpose and have much lower fees than full-service plans.

Regular landline phone service is much more complicated than it used to be. Post the hours of free or discounted long-distance calling by each telephone so all family members can help save on the phone bill. Check into flat-rate plans that let you call anywhere in the country anytime for a reasonable monthly fee. Just make sure that everyone knows that the free-call feature only applies within the country. A friend of mine recently called Iran, talked for about fifteen minutes, and was surprised to get a $70 bill.

Another way to save money on long-distance service from your home phone is to buy cheap telephone calling cards, available at most discount stores. The card entitles you to a certain number of prepaid minutes and provides an access numbers that you dial before you dial the phone number you are calling. The cost per minute with these cards can sometimes be a fraction of the cost of using your regular long-distance company.

27. Utilities

Utilities are like a slow leak in our finances if we don't stay vigilant about energy usage. The cause-and-effect of most energy use is often hard to see. Some things that we think will save money turn out to be inconsequential, and others are energy hogs. For example, did you know that, according to the Alliance to Save Energy, you pay over three times the initial cost of an air-conditioning unit over its lifetime for the energy to run it?

The Alliance to Save Energy has a website called Energy Hog (www .energyhog.org) that tells you dozens of ways you can save energy. Many of the ideas don't cost anything to implement. For example:

- Lower the temperature of your water heater to 120 degrees or lower.

- In hot weather, pull the shades on the windows that the sun comes in. When it cools down at night, open screened windows to let in cool, fresh air.

- Where the amount of light from a light fixture is not a high priority, use lower-wattage bulbs.

- Wash most clothing in cold water and save up to $63 a year on your energy bill.

- Check your furnace or air-conditioning filters every month. Dirty filters make your appliances work harder.

Your local utility company may provide a free analysis of your home and ways that you can save energy. Some utilities even have programs that provide free or low-cost weatherproofing of homes. For more information, see chapter 13.

28. Vacations, trips

People are traveling now more than ever. It seems like people used to save for years and go to Hawaii on their twenty-fifth wedding anniversary. Now they are likely to go every year. If you work with many people who have two-income budgets, you may have to endure tales of Paris, the Caribbean, and every island in Hawaii until your idea of camping in the nearest national park sounds pretty lame. Doesn't everybody go on at least one cruise a year these days?

Now that you know that the average American family is deep in debt, and that the national savings rate was actually *negative* in 2005, you have to wonder if they all should be flying off to exotic locations as much as they do. In fact, if they are piling these trips onto their already heavy burdened credit cards, they are probably creating more stress for themselves than any vacation can help.

When I was growing up, most people I knew talked about vacations to their grandma's house or to the nearby coast. Camping was also popular. A few kids got to fly to Disneyland—an adventure so huge they had to tell the rest of us about it in show-and-tell. We didn't feel deprived that we couldn't fly to a resort in Puerto Vallarta for spring break. (We had never heard of Puerto Vallarta!)

The truth is, you don't necessarily have more fun the farther you get from home. Most of us haven't fully explored the area within a day's drive of our house. We can find local festivals, museums, art galleries, and tourist stops without getting on an airplane. Or we can get in our car or on a train and venture farther without maxing out our credit cards. Consider these ideas for budget vacations:

- Go camping. Most kids love camping. Leave the electronics at home, bring some card games, and enjoy some together time. Cook over a fire—everything tastes better outdoors.

- When you travel, bring your own food so you don't have to eat in restaurants for every meal. Eating out is more fun if you don't do it three times a day.

- If you want to try a more expensive restaurant, try it at lunchtime. The food is just as good, and the prices are sometimes half what they are later.

- Go to relatives' houses. Help with the extra food costs, of course, but don't turn down the offer of the spare room or the couch in the den.

- Make them come to you. Offer to host a family reunion at your house or at a park near you. Or give visiting friends or relatives a tour of the local sights. It's more fun to look at your hometown landmarks when you have someone to show them to.

Give yourself credit!

If you've made it this far, it's time for a break! You've accomplished a lot. Sometimes it's not easy to plan a realistic budget that works. If you share your finances with someone but you worked on this budget by yourself, now's the time to show that person what you've come up with and get him or her to buy in on the plan. You can't make much progress on this project together unless you first come to an agreement on where you are going and how you plan to get there.

13 Pay the Rent and Utilities

The bills you've gotta pay,
no matter what

It doesn't pay to skip the rent or the water bill. Rent and utilities should be the first bills you pay. Pay them even if you can't pay anything else. You can put off paying your credit card bills if you must, you can get food at the local food pantry, and you might be able to ride your bicycle to work, but you need a warm, safe place to live— and that puts rent and utilities right at the top of the list.

If you can't pay your rent and utilities, you can face escalating efforts at collection from your landlord and the utility companies— starting at collection letters and phone calls and moving eventually to threats, service cutoffs, and eviction. In the long term, your credit suffers, and you may have a hard time getting either utility service or an apartment.

Another reason to stay current on your rent is that it is much harder to find a good rental at a fair price once you have a history of not paying your rent. I know a woman who pays about $400 a month more to rent a house than any person with good credit would pay. She had to go with the only landlord who would take someone with her history of not paying rent and being evicted, and that landlord knew that he could charge her whatever he wanted. It doesn't seem like a fair thing to do to someone who's already down. From the landlord's point of view though, if he's going to take that kind of risk, he wants to get paid for it.

If you absolutely cannot pay your rent or utilities, you may be able to get help or a reprieve. As with all bills, the worst thing you can do is ignore them. You may be able to find help or at least buy time if you know what your options are.

Utility bills

Missing one month's bill

If you miss paying a utility bill one month, nothing much is likely to happen. Your next bill will show two months' worth, and if you pay it then, that's the end of it. Some utility companies allow so little time between the date they send out the bills and the due date for payments that they must get a good share of their payments after the due date anyway. Most of them don't even charge a late fee, or the late fee is very small.

Avoiding cutoffs and reconnection fees

If you make a habit of paying late, or if you miss two or more payments, you will get notices in the mail that sound more and more serious. If they say that your service is going to be cut off, don't doubt it. Do whatever it takes to avoid a disconnection; it's a lot easier to keep utilities turned on than it is to get service again once they're disconnected. Not only do utility companies charge reconnection fees, but they may require a deposit of up to three times your average bill before they reconnect you.

Utility companies don't like to disconnect people's services. However, if they don't get paid and they don't hear from you, they don't have a choice. If you don't have the money for your utilities, call the company and explain the situation. Be prepared to give a reason why you are behind in your payments, such as unemployment or extended illness. If your income is simply too low, say so.

Instead of just saying that you can't pay the bill, say how much per month you can pay now, and when you expect to be able to catch up on payments.

Check out utility assistance programs

If you are currently living on a relatively low income, or if you are in an emergency situation where you could have your heat turned off, the federal Low Income Home Energy Assistance Program (LIHEAP) may be able to help you. The Department of Health and Human Services (DHHS) funds this program, and it is administered by individual states and some nonprofit agencies. Although the rules vary depending on where you live, all LIHEAP programs are designed to help people with their home heating and cooling bills and to help them weatherize their homes so they can save on heating and cooling expenses.

LIHEAP won't solve all your utility bill troubles; it is designed only to help with heating bills, not to pay them in their entirety. Under some LIHEAP programs, you can get help with your electricity bill *or* your natural gas bill, but not both. If they help with electricity, they pay enough to help with the cost of electricity for hot water heating, refrigeration, or cooking, but not for "nonessential" uses, such as lighting.

LIHEAP programs have limited funding, so they must decide which families have the highest need. Families with the highest energy needs receive the most help, and energy needs are determined by factors such as your family size, the ages of your family members, and the cost of heating and cooling where you live. Some LIHEAP programs automatically help any household that gets Temporary Assistance for Needy Families (TANF), Supplemental Security Income (SSI), food stamps, or certain veterans' benefits that are based on need.

Besides giving direct help with heating and cooling bills, LIHEAP programs can help you make your home more energy efficient. A few energy-saving measures may save you up to 30% on your monthly bills—and your home will feel warmer and less drafty. Ask the people at LIHEAP about their Weatherization Program, which may provide improvements such as attic insulation, weatherstripping, and minor repairs at little or no cost to you.

For more information, see the LIHEAP Web site at http://www .acf.dhhs.gov/programs/liheap, or find the link to LIHEAP programs in your state at http://www.acf.hhs.gov/programs/liheap/ grantees/states.html. Some states even offer their application forms online; check out http://liheap.ncat.org/admin.htm#applications.

Many electric companies also repair or replace older service equipment in homes or mobile homes at little or no cost to you. New, more efficient equipment can help you stay warmer and have lower utility bills as well.

Utility bill averaging

Another program that may help you, especially if your utilities are much higher in the winter months, is utility bill averaging. Under this plan, you pay the same monthly utility bill all year, generally using a formula based on the previous year's bills. This makes budgeting your money much easier and avoids the shock of opening a bill for January's heat that's almost as high as your rent.

State laws protecting utility customers

If you live in a state with cold winters, your state probably has laws protecting you from arbitrary cutoff of your heating utilities during the winter months. These laws don't pay the bill for you, but they may keep the heat on so you and your family don't freeze. Some laws have special protections for households with elderly or disabled residents or infants. Check with the Public Utilities Commission for your state.

Rent

If the power goes out, especially when it's cold, it's inconvenient. If the water is turned off and the toilets no longer work, you might decide to go stay with relatives. If you don't pay your rent, however, you can find yourself and everything you own literally out on the sidewalk. Eviction is one thing you want to avoid if at all possible.

What an eviction looks like

Events depicted in movies and on television seldom bear any resemblance to real life. You may have seen film evictions where the sheriff nails a notice to the door and his lackey throws everything a family owns out onto the sidewalk, while the neighbors jeer at the sheriff and the bad guys take off with any china and household goods that don't break when they hit the pavement. That's how it looks in the movies, anyway.

In real life, evictions are not nearly as exciting. The effect is much the same, however. The people I've known who have been evicted really did find themselves on the sidewalk with all their belongings. Instead of nailing a notice to the door, the sheriff used tape. Instead of throwing dishes and knickknacks onto the sidewalk, the people working for the apartment owner threw everything into large trash bags—which they put on the sidewalk. They didn't pad the dishes, so the result wasn't much different. A few neighbors and sightseers gathered around, but it was fairly quiet.

One resourceful woman, Eve, used the day of her eviction to have a big garage sale in the parking lot of the apartment complex. The apartment managers couldn't stop her; after all, they were the ones who hauled all her stuff out there. A friend stopped by and offered to take her houseplants temporarily. Her son decided to go stay with a friend for a while. Eve sold what she could, stuffed her car as full as she could, and drove away.

After Jon was evicted, he also found himself sitting on the sidewalk, surrounded by his entertainment system and other belongings. He couldn't get it all in his car, and he knew that if he left it for a moment unattended, it would disappear. So he sat there, despondently guarding his stuff. Fortunately, a friend driving by saw Jon and stopped. He went back to get a truck, and together they loaded everything up.

As harsh as eviction is, it's during hard times like these that people discover the compassionate, generous nature of others. Eve spent a few nights in her car, but most nights she found one friend or another who would let her stay over. Jon stayed with the friend who had found him sitting on the sidewalk with everything he owned. Eventually, each found a new apartment.

Many tenants think that if they get behind in their rent and get evicted, they don't have to pay the back rent they owed to their landlord, but back rent is a bill like any other. It will show up on their credit report, and, like any other creditor, their old landlord can take steps to get paid, including using a collection agency, going to small claims court, putting liens on property, and even garnishing wages. The rent doesn't go away just because they've moved.

After a person has been evicted, it is very difficult to find landlords willing to rent to him. They will want a reference from his last landlord, and when that landlord tells them that he was evicted for nonpayment of rent, his application will go to the bottom of the stack, if not to the trash bin. Landlords even have special credit bureaus, called tenant screening agencies, to track bad tenant risks. We can't blame the landlords—they can't afford to pay the mortgage and other expenses and not receive rent when it is due. The fact remains that no matter how far behind you are and how nasty the landlord is, you are better off working with him or at least leaving on good terms than you are allowing yourself to be evicted.

Working with the landlord and avoiding eviction

If you can't pay your rent when it's due, you have some time before you have to worry about eviction. Depending on state law, you may have weeks or months before the sheriff shows up at your door. Don't waste any of the time you have. Use that time to catch up on your rent, negotiate something with your landlord, or find some other place to live. The worst thing you can do is to live in denial and do nothing, thinking that your landlord won't evict you. He will!

If you are having a hard time paying your rent because of a temporary situation such as unemployment or illness, talk to your landlord and suggest a temporary reduction in your rent. The harder it is to find renters in your area, the better your chances of success. Unless renters are very hard to come by, your landlord will probably insist that you make up the rest of the rent when you do find employment or your financial situation otherwise improves, but at least you should be able to stay in your home.

Say you talk to your landlord and he agrees to lower your rent by 25% until you find another job. You promise to pay the rest back in higher rent payments, beginning one month after you begin working. You're happy with the reduced rent burden, and your landlord is happy because he doesn't have to evict you and start looking for someone new. So you're all set, right?

People have misunderstandings all too often. You might have thought he meant one thing, but he thought another. Both of you assumed you would find a job soon—but what happens if finding a job takes longer? Write a letter to your landlord. Thank him for being understanding, and write out exactly what you both agreed to. Keep a copy of the letter, of course.

After you have reached an agreement, the landlord can't evict you as long as you hold up your end of the deal. Make it your top priority. If you have to sell something, do temporary work, or take out a loan—do whatever it takes. You can do without almost anything else, but you must have a place to live.

Finding a less expensive alternative

When you can't afford your rent, the simplest solution is to try to move into a cheaper place owned by the same landlord. If you live in an apartment complex, for example, your landlord may be happy to let you move from a two-bedroom apartment to a one-bedroom unit or even to a studio. You save the time and trouble of finding and applying for an apartment and the expense of moving farther away. If you are unemployed, you may have a difficult time finding a new landlord who will take someone without demonstrable adequate income. Your current landlord knows you, and hopefully knows that you are a good, responsible tenant worth keeping, so he may be more willing to work with you.

Another option is to find a place elsewhere, perhaps in a different part of town or even in a different state. In the Seattle area, rents near the high-tech business districts are outrageously expensive. Many people commute an hour or more to work because they get more house for their money in the outlying areas. In some places like California, where you would have to drive a prohibitive distance to find lower rents, some people pack up and move to another state to find a place they can afford on what they make.

So many people have moved to places with a lower cost of living that many popular magazines have written articles on this trend. Some people are moving back to places where they grew up. Perhaps they were from Kansas City, but they were drawn to the excitement of San Francisco as young adults. When they start having children, they sometimes realize that they have a choice: both work full-time, live in a small apartment, and just scrape by in the beautiful Bay Area; or move to a place where they can still comfortably buy a house with a yard, on one income. As a bonus, sometimes they are nearer their kids' grandparents and other family members. It's amazing how much less stress you have when you don't have to spend all your energy working to pay exorbitant rent.

If you have lived in the same apartment or the same neighborhood for a long time, moving can be a scary thing. I've moved thirteen times as an adult, and I know how unsettling it can feel, especially moving from state to state and starting all over finding friends, doctors, and favorite stores. Finding a new hairdresser was sometimes the scariest part! There is something to like in every new place, though, and there is nothing to stop you from going back to your old neighborhood sometime in the future. You do whatever it takes to survive, so you might as well consider all your options—including moving.

Exchanging services for rent

Eve, the woman who had a garage sale the day she was evicted from her apartment, found another apartment after about six weeks of looking and saving her money. Unfortunately, her troubles continued when she was laid off and ran out of unemployment benefits. Eve was thinking ahead this time, however. She noticed the services that her landlord was paying for around the complex, from landscape maintenance to cleaning, and offered to work in exchange for rent. This worked out well for both her and her landlord, and eventually she took on some assistant manager duties as well.

Maintenance work and property management are time-tested ways people earn free or reduced rent in exchange for work. Don't assume that being an apartment manager or assistant manager is an easy task, however. Other tenants may expect you to open locked doors, settle noise complaints, and call repairmen at all hours of the day and night. Many people have a new respect for the rent that landlords and managers earn when they see what they have to do to earn it.

Sharing rent

It may make sense for you to share the rent with someone, either temporarily or for the long term. If you are single, maybe you can rent out a room or two, or you might find someone who has a place and is willing to rent to you. Multiple families can even share a home, and in some parts of the country where prices are high in comparison to wages, this arrangement is not unusual.

If you live near a college, you shouldn't have trouble finding one or more students to rent a room. You can advertise on the school bulletin board or in the school newspaper.

Screen your applicants carefully, and never fail to check references—especially if you will be sharing any common living spaces. You'll be getting to know your new roommate very well after he or she moves in.

Be sure to check your rental agreement to make sure that you aren't violating any rules. Before anyone moves in, set ground rules, such as what time you expect the house to be quiet and your policies on alcohol, parties, and house guests. If you plan ahead, sharing rent can ease your financial burden considerably.

Can my landlord get rid of me without going through with an eviction?

What if you've done your best, you haven't found another place to live, and your landlord wants you out *now*? State laws vary, but they all contain protections for tenants. Your landlord can rant all he wants, but if he wants to evict you, he has to follow the eviction procedures for your state, which can take weeks or months. Generally, he must file a lawsuit to evict you and obtain a court order. He can't make you move by locking you out, turning off your utilities, seizing things that belong to you, or threatening you.

Legal and charitable help to prevent eviction

If your landlord has filed an eviction lawsuit or may be planning to do so, you need to find help immediately. Many areas have nonprofit organizations or government help for people who are in danger of being evicted. For example, the Eviction Prevention Program in New York City helps families get emergency money for back rent from the Human Resource Administration (HRA) and from charitable organizations. It also provides legal help during housing court proceedings and in dealings with landlords.

To find help where you live, you can type "avoid eviction" and your city and state into an Internet a search engine or go to a social services department in your city. If you belong to a church or other religious organization, it may have a community needs fund for such emergencies, and some even give comprehensive help and counseling to help you get back on your feet.

14 Pay or Get Help with Medical Bills

Facing one of the biggest causes of financial distress

When Joy and Ben were working their way through college, they had barely enough money to get by every month. They were young and healthy, and they thought they could do without medical insurance until they graduated. Besides, who could afford the premiums? Then Ben went to the emergency room with sharp pains in his side. Surgery for a ruptured appendix saved his life, but before Ben could go back to work he found himself facing a hospital bill larger than his annual pay.

Joy and Ben cleaned out their savings account to pay as much as they could on the hospital bill, but it didn't help much. Joy went down to the hospital to see if they qualified for any government help and to work out a payment plan. To Joy's surprise, the clerk at the hospital told her that she would have qualified for government aid—if she hadn't already made payments. Now that Joy had started paying off the bill, the clerk said, she would have to pay the whole thing.

Medical bills, by their sheer size, can sometimes overwhelm even the most careful planners. Help is available, but the criteria and processes for getting it sometimes defy common sense. What you do when you first get the bill can make a big difference. Take these steps to deal with your medical bills:

Step 1. Make sure the bill is right

Some experts say that 90% of hospital bills have significant errors, very few of which are in the patient's favor. Some of the bills are almost funny, like the charges for after-childbirth care for a middle-aged man, or the $126 charge for mucous removal system—apparently a box of Kleenex. It's not funny, however, when it's your bill and you get charged $5 for one nonprescription pain pill, or you get charged for services you never received and double-charged for some services you did receive.

I remember when I was in the hospital to have my daughter, someone came around passing out bags with small packages of goodies for mothers with new babies. They looked like samples to me, and since the lady didn't ask me if I wanted it, I just smiled and thanked her. Most of it was stuff I would never use, but I was trying to be nice. Imagine my surprise when my hospital bill showed a $25 charge for the bag of personal care items! What a racket—nobody asked me if I wanted the bag, and none of the items were for use in the hospital. Somebody had found a way to sell a few dollars' worth of supplies to a captive audience for a grossly inflated price. The sad thing is, I paid for it without saying a word to the hospital. I was young and I thought they knew more than I did—who was I to question the way they did things?

When you get your bill, go through every line and make sure you understand what each item is for. The medical center must give you an itemized bill, and if it uses indecipherable codes and abbreviations, the billing office must explain to you what they stand for. Ideally, when you were receiving treatment you kept a list of the pills you took and the treatments you received. If you don't recognize something, mark it and insist on an explanation.

Whether you stay in the hospital or have outpatient medical treatment, you get bills from all kinds of doctors, anesthesiologists, labs, technicians, and other people whose names you have never even heard before. Examine each line item on their bills.

If you aren't sure who someone is, ask your doctor if it is someone he authorized to provide a service. Never pay someone if you aren't sure the charges are legitimate. A common scam is sending bills for fake lab tests and other services to the elderly and to people who have been in the hospital, hoping that their bills will be paid without question. One woman, Gladys, received such a bill and would have paid it if her daughter hadn't asked her what it was for. She called the doctor and discovered that the bill was a hoax. No such lab existed, and the doctor had not ordered the services. Gladys had just figured that since she had many medical bills, anything that came in the mail must be all right.

Step 2. Seek help

As Joy and Ben discovered, the time to seek help with a medical bill is before too much time has gone by, and before you drain your savings account to start paying for it. If you are faced with a bill that you don't see how you can pay, immediately contact your hospital's collection department and ask what private and government help is available.

You may also find help on your own. Investigate charitable and religious organizations that help people negotiate and pay medical bills; some are set up specially to serve veterans, children, cancer patients, HIV/AIDS patients, or other special cases or populations.

Step 3. Negotiate your bill

Hospitals, doctors' offices, and other medical service suppliers are generally as pragmatic about collecting money as any other business. They have nothing to gain by trying to get money from someone who simply doesn't have it; in fact, they hate to waste too much time and money trying to do so. They would rather get some money than

none, and they dislike having accounts receivable cases open indefinitely. Sending accounts to collection agencies is not a great solution
for them, either, because the collection agency gets a large cut of any
payments it collects.

If you owe a substantial amount for medical services, the best
thing you can do is to make an appointment with the person in
charge of collections and go in and honestly explain your situation.
Be prepared. Bring a written list with your basic financial information: how much income you get per month and your total living expenses, including other debt payments. If you have insurance, bring
proof that the bill has been submitted to the insurance company, any
communications you have received from the insurance company,
and the amount you expect the insurance company to pay.

Tell her that you are willing to work out a solution to the problem. Tell her how much you think you can pay per month—don't
make her guess.

Specifically ask for relief from interest, penalties, and collection
services. Ask her to delay sending your account to a collection service and not to send negative information to the credit bureaus.
Many times, you only get what you ask for. When creditors see that
you are not avoiding them and that you are willing to do the best
you can, they are much more likely to help you.

While drama and exaggerations won't help, don't be afraid to explain your situation. If you cannot go back to work right away,
that's a factor she should know. If the stress of collection activity
may affect your recovery, mention that. If the person you are talking
to does not respond, ask to speak to a department head. Some hospitals even have patient representatives who can help you resolve
your case. Someone on staff should be able to help you.

The result you should hope for from a hospital or other medical
facility is a negotiated reduction in the amount you owe. This is one
reason it is important to negotiate before you start paying. Say you
owe $50,000, which you obviously cannot pay anytime soon out of
your current income. Say that you can round up $10,000 by draining

your savings, borrowing from your dad, or selling your second car. After you pay $10,000 of the $50,000 bill, it will be harder to negotiate with the hospital on the rest. If, on the other hand, you go to the collections department and offer to pay $10,000 in a lump sum in exchange for a reduced balance, they may be willing to settle for that.

Doctor bills can mount up, too, even if you never check into a hospital. If you have chronic or multiple conditions, you may find yourself facing more in doctor bills than you know how to pay. Especially if you need continuing care from your doctor, you need to make sure that your bill stays current or that other arrangements have been agreed to. As with hospital bills, make an appointment and go talk to the person in charge of collections at your doctor's office. If your doctor works at a larger clinic, that person may not be the person at the front desk in your doctor's office; it may be someone on another floor or in another building. Tell him your situation, including how much you can pay and how much you expect insurance to pay. Doctors routinely write off portions of patients' bills, especially when the patients make good faith efforts to pay.

One thing you should know when you are dealing with medical bills is that not everyone who goes into the office pays the same rate. It's like flying on an airplane—different passengers pay different rates depending on how they got their ticket. In a doctor's office, one person may pay $120 for an office visit, the person sitting next to her may get a discount and pay $97, and another may belong to a plan with a negotiated rate of $75. When the doctor treats someone whose care is paid for by the government, she may get paid much less than that. Ironically, the person who pays cash for doctors' visits often pays the highest rate because everyone else pays a rate negotiated by an outside party.

Knowing that doctors can and do reduce their rates can help you feel more confident about asking for a lowered rate yourself. If you feel funny about asking for a "discount," try asking if you can pay the rate the office gives to people who have insurance. If you already have a large bill at your doctor's, it's not too late to point out that you didn't get a negotiated rate and that if you did, you would be able to make better progress on your bill. Of course, you need to make a conscientious effort to pay your bill; the office isn't likely to help if you don't hold up your end of the deal.

Step 4—last resort only: bankruptcy

If you have followed steps 1 through 3 and you still have insurmountable medical bills that you cannot find a way to mitigate or pay, you may want to consider bankruptcy.

As discussed in chapter 4, bankruptcy is not a quick fix-all solution. It's expensive—by the time you pay legal expenses and trustee fees, it will cost a lot more than the advertised price you see in bankruptcy ads. That's money out of your pocket or from your assets that doesn't help pay your bills or do anything but pay the people who facilitate your bankruptcy. Furthermore, you can lose things that are important to you, such as family heirlooms and valuable collections, in a bankruptcy. Bankruptcy trustees don't generally auction off your personal effects like you've seen in old movies, but they do have the power to seize jewelry, cars, motor homes, and other assets to pay your bills. Bankruptcy isn't likely to alleviate your stress level in the short term—not with the paperwork, loss of control over your finances, and embarrassment that inevitably come with it.

However, medical bills can be wiped out by a Chapter 7 bankruptcy. Many bills, such as taxes, child support, and student loans, normally survive bankruptcy, but medical bills are almost always discharged. In fact, medical bills are one of the main reasons that bankruptcy laws exist, because the courts recognize the impossibility of paying off enormous medical bills on an average person's income level.

If you think that bankruptcy is the only answer to your medical bill problem, be sure to seek qualified legal services. Bankruptcy is not a do-it-yourself project, nor is it best done by fly-by-night operators or the cheapest service in town. Find a reputable lawyer and ask him what your options are, and if his advice makes sense, follow it.

Chapter 7, Chapter 13, and medical bills

A Chapter 7 bankruptcy uses your assets to pay as much as possible to your creditors in a court-prescribed order and wipes out any debts, including medical bills, you have left. A Chapter 13 bankruptcy may wipe out some of your debts, but it allows the court to set up a payment plan for you to pay off your debts usually in three to five years. Under the new bankruptcy laws, more people with average or above-average income are required to file Chapter 13 and to pay off their debts over time.

Mistakes to avoid when you have medical bills

- **Don't pay medical bills off with another loan before you try to negotiate.** If you take out a home equity loan or any other loan to pay off your medical bills, you can no longer negotiate with the medical facility on the amount of your bill. The bank won't negotiate on the amount it has paid to the hospital. Negotiate your bill first; then look for a low-interest source of money to pay your reduced bill.

- **Don't put medical bills on your high-interest credit card.** Almost any creditor is better than a credit card company for holding large debts. Credit card companies often charge unconscionable interest rates, and who's to stop yours from raising the rates after you put a huge bill on your card? If the hospital charges interest, it may be a fraction of the rate the credit card company charges. Credit card companies are also quick to report to credit bureaus the next time you miss a payment. Given the choice, I'd rather have a mark from a hospital than from a credit card company on my credit report.

- **Don't take money out of your retirement plans to pay medical bills.** In times of hardship, you may want to reduce the amount you are contributing to your retirement plans temporarily. However, money you have contributed to your IRA, 401(k) or 403(b) plan, or any other retirement plan should stay there until you are ready to retire. You need that money for retirement, and if you take it out now, you will have a hard time replacing it. Also, depending on the plan, you may have to pay tax and penalties on the amount you withdraw. The biggest reason that you should not withdraw money from your retirement accounts to pay bills is that your retirement accounts are generally safe from creditors. The laws vary by state, but a retirement account is one of the safest places you can keep your money.

- **Don't avoid the problem and stop opening the bills.** It might be easier in the short run to quit looking at bills you don't think you can pay, but that's the worst way to deal with them. As with any other bills, the only way to solve them is to face them head on.

Kari's story

I met a young woman named Kari who was haunted by the hospital bills she owed. She hadn't told anyone in the office about the terrible car accident she'd been in—an accident that took her sister's life. One day when everyone else was at lunch, she confided to me that all day, every day, she sat at her desk with a knot in her stomach, just thinking about the bills she couldn't pay. She had gone off the road and rolled her car, been airlifted to the nearest hospital, and stayed one night under observation. Her total bill was over three times her annual salary. She couldn't see how it could have cost that much, and she saw no possible way to ever pay it. She remembers telling the emergency workers that she couldn't afford the airlift, and she remembers them telling her not to worry about it. Well, now it was time to worry about it.

I asked her if she had ever seen a detailed hospital bill, and she said no. She didn't know how much of the bill was the airlift and how much was actual medical care, or even if the bill was right. The accident was eight months earlier, and she had never talked to a representative of the hospital or sought aid of any kind. Every time she got mail from the hospital, she got a queasy feeling—even though she no longer opened any of the envelopes.

Kari's reaction was far from unusual. The horror of the accident was too painful to bear. Dealing with an impossible hospital bill brought back all those memories and the loss of her sister again. Even if she were to face it, she didn't know where to go or who to talk to. So she just waited day after day, month after month, with this terrible secret.

I encouraged Kari to take steps to solve this problem, and the last time I talked to her, she was making progress. She had looked on the hospital's Web site, and she was making an appointment to talk to the collections department. Kari was also planning to ask for a copy of an itemized bill, especially since the total seemed awfully high for the amount of time she was in the hospital. Given the outrageous size of Kari's bill and her demonstrable lack of resources to pay it, the hospital should be able to work something out to resolve her case.

Don't give up

Medical bills are one of the biggest contributors to financial hardship and personal bankruptcies in this country. We have arguably the best medical care in the world, but it's also among the most expensive, and we don't get to choose when we need it.

You have several reasons not to give up when you have big medical bills, however. For one thing, you are not the first person to ring up medical bills far in excess of your ability to pay. If in addition you are sick and your income is lowered because you cannot work full-time, other people have been in this situation, too. Hospitals, doctors' offices, labs, and other medical facilities deal with these financial problems every day, and they want to resolve them. They know that some bills are uncollectible, and they have a budget, and generally outside assistance, to help with these bills—but you have to ask. By taking the steps in this chapter, you can face your past medical bills and stop spending so much energy worrying about them.

15

Pay Child Support and Alimony

When other people are counting on you

Every story has two sides. In divorce and child support stories, the husbands and fathers seem to come out looking bad more often than not. If you go to an Internet search engine and type in something like "child support" or "alimony," the vast majority of the results you get will be written from the mother's point of view and explain how to collect child support and alimony, and even how to use extreme measures to do so. If you type the keywords "father's rights," you get a few results from the dad's point of view, but you also find blatantly negative articles and some that seem to view all ex-husbands and noncustodial fathers as deadbeats, if not criminals.

A Note on Word Choice

Although many women pay child support and alimony, many more men still do so. In this chapter, for convenience I refer to the non-custodial parent or the ex-spouse paying alimony as a male, while recognizing that many women face the same issues.

Men are sometimes afraid to tell their stories because of the presumption that they must be the guilty party, or the "bad dad." When people get a chance to hear the other side of the story, they hear something different. They hear about men who can be taken advantage of, by women who may or may not have had kids with them. They hear about men trying to support two or three families after a series of failed relationships. They find out about men who love their kids and want to do the right thing but are caught in circumstances that make that almost impossible.

Both women and men are capable of causing marriage breakups. Studies show that two-thirds of divorces involving children are initiated by women. Some courts order child support and alimony payments that are unfair and don't leave the paying ex-spouse enough to live on. Sometimes, men can hit hard times financially and need a temporary reprieve.

These are most common complaints from payers of child support and alimony:

- The court-ordered payments are too high, causing an unfair burden.

- The father needs relief from payment because of financial hardship, such as illness or unemployment.

- The mother is irresponsible. She may neglect the children or vindictively keep them from their father, or she may have a substance abuse problem.

- The payments are unwarranted; for example, the man doesn't believe the child is his.

You can do something about high or unfair support orders. First, you need to understand some basics about support and how it is determined.

Contest high court-ordered payments

Court-ordered payments are sometimes unreasonably high simply because the courts do not have all the information they need. They often use default formulas that are not necessarily fair in every case. If you are required to make support payments that seem impossibly high, your plan of action depends on where you are in the separation and divorce process.

Temporary orders

If you are recently separated, you may be liable for child and spousal support for the time between the separation and the final divorce decree, via a temporary order. The temporary order can be established by default, by a consent order, or by a hearing order.

- **Default temporary support court orders.** You should try to avoid a default court order. A default court order is the one that the child support agency will establish for you, without your input. It will almost certainly not be in your favor.

  Default support orders are not necessarily reasonable. They may be based on the amount the mother or estranged spouse is receiving in government assistance, or they may be the amount she requests. Sometimes the order is for more than a person earns.

  With any financial problem, the worst thing you can do is ignore the first signs of trouble, but this is especially true with a court-ordered default support order. If you get a notice from an agency saying that it is establishing a default order for child support or alimony, you must respond immediately. If you don't respond, the agency assumes that the amount it establishes is correct and you legally owe the full amount. You could be unemployed or disabled, and the agency could have established the amount based on what you earned at a previous job—no matter. If you don't stand up for yourself, you owe the money by default.

If you don't dispute the order right away, you may be able to get it modified at a later date. Unfortunately, the amount is generally modified from that point forward; you will still owe the amount that has been adding up until that point.

- **Consent or agreed order for temporary support.** If you respond to the notice you receive within the allowed time, you may be able to work out a consent order (also called an agreed order) for temporary support. Because you have input, a consent order is much more likely to be realistic. Both sides are motivated to negotiate and agree on an order because it saves the time and considerable expense of going to court for a formal hearing.

- **Hearing order for temporary support.** If you respond, but you and the other party cannot work out a temporary support agreement, you have the right to a hearing. A judge or hearings officer will listen to both sides, look at financial documents and other evidence, and make a decision. This can go either way, depending on the judge. You are usually better off negotiating a consent order whenever possible.

The amount of the temporary support order is generally calculated using a predetermined schedule that takes into account the man's income, or both parties' income, and the number of children. The amount may be increased or reduced; for example, if a child has special needs, more support may be required to care for him. The amount may also include past-due amounts, which are sometimes calculated from the time of the separation, but may be calculated from the time one party applied for government assistance or asked for agency help collecting support.

When past support is being assessed, you should bring up anything that would reduce the amount you would have been obligated to pay during that time. For example, if your income was lower, you should provide evidence to the other party or the court. You should also get credit for support you have provided in the interim, such as cash, house payments, medical insurance, and clothing for the children.

You may be able to negotiate on your monthly temporary support order by offering to pay more for monthly support in exchange for a reduction in the past-due amount. This is only a good idea if you expect the divorce to finalize soon; otherwise, you may end up paying more.

Establishment of divorce decree

The permanent divorce decree is much more important than the temporary order because you will be living with the decree much longer. The divorce decree covers all aspects of the divorce, from alimony and child support to visitation and the division of assets. Here are some things you should know about permanent support:

- **Fixed amount.** A fixed-amount support order remains the same regardless of your financial circumstances. If your income goes down or you lose your job, you must file for relief or you will be obligated to keep paying the full amount regardless of your income. On the other hand, if your income goes up, your ex-spouse doesn't automatically receive more money without filing for an adjustment.

- **Percentage amount.** If your income varies by season or from year to year, it may be to your advantage to have the amount of support determined as a percentage of your income rather than as a flat amount. You generally have to pay a minimum amount regardless of your income level. This method is more trouble for the agencies and courts to track because they must continually document your income level. However, this method is probably the most fair for both parties.

- **Employed vs. unemployed order.** Another way to figure the amount of support when your employment is not always regular is to specify two amounts: one for when you are working, and one for when you are not.

- **Escalator clauses.** An escalator clause is an addition to a support order that stipulates a rise in the support amount over time. For example, the support amount may rise each year with inflation, using the federal government inflation numbers. It's not usually in your favor to have automatic escalator clauses, because your income may not rise at the same rate that inflation does. If you must have an escalator clause, try to agree on an annual cap on the percentage the support amount can be raised.

- **Age of majority.** Not all decrees assume children will stop receiving child support on their eighteenth birthday. Realistically, most eighteen-year-olds are still in high school, and as they get close to graduation, their expenses tend to accelerate rather than slow down. The decree may stipulate that child support continues until the child graduates from high school, joins the military, or gets married. Some decrees require support to continue through college or at least until the child reaches age twenty-one. It is better not to have college support written into your decree even if you plan to put your kids through college, because you cannot foresee what your circumstances will be. What if your child goes through a stage where he doesn't get passing grades—will you be required to keep paying tuition? In addition, your children are more likely to appreciate your help if they know that it is voluntary and not ordered by a court.

- **IRS dependency exemptions.** To avoid future conflict, the divorce decree should specify whether you can claim the dependency exemption for one or more of the children on your tax return. It may even be worth negotiating to pay slightly more support and receive the tax benefits. For more information, talk to a tax professional or read Publication 17, *Your Federal Income Tax*, on the IRS Web site at http://www .irs.gov/publications/p17/index.html.

It's up to you and your attorney to make sure your interests are represented and the support orders are reasonable. Don't let anyone make you feel guilty about not wanting to sign all your money, present and future, away. You can always give your children or your ex-spouse more than the court orders; your priority now is to make sure that you can survive financially. Think about your future, too. You don't know how things may change—you could someday have a new family you need to support, or your health or career may not go as planned. Don't throw up your hands and agree to anything just to have this painful experience over with. You will regret it later.

CAUTION: Many people in the midst of a divorce also find themselves stressed out over their career as well. They may be tempted to quit their job or take one that pays a lot less, thinking that they will have to pay less support that way. After all, the courts can't make people keep jobs they hate, can they? Actually, they can and they do. An unsympathetic court can order you to pay support based on what you have made in the past, which may be more than your total pay if you suddenly switch careers.

Get hardship relief

The expectation that men can and should always make full child support and alimony payments on time is simplistic. Of course, children can't skip eating this month because their parents are short on money, but some allowance must be made for hard times. When the family was intact, they could all adjust to financial ups and downs. If a parent's business slowed, or if the car needed expensive repairs, the family could put off expenditures, take a cheaper vacation, and make do. When things got better, they could eat out more often and live more comfortably.

After a divorce, unless the decree had some provision for income fluctuations and periods of unemployment, men are expected to keep paying as if they are still receiving a paycheck. That's not realistic.

Modification of the divorce decree because of unemployment, illness, and other hardships

If you lose your job or become disabled, you may assume that the amount of support you must pay is automatically or retroactively lowered to a reasonable level. You can't pay more than your income, of course. However, unless you take legal steps to reduce the support amount, it stays the same. If you wait until you get around to filing for a reduced amount, even if you can change the amount you have to pay from that time on, you still generally owe the full amount of past-due payments. Don't think that telling your ex-spouse about your situation gets you off the hook, even if she assures you that it's all right to pay less until you go back to work. If your financial situation changes drastically, you must take legal action immediately to protect yourself.

In most states, you can get a support modification in one of two ways: You can petition the court for a modification and have a court hearing to determine the new support amount, or you and your ex-spouse can fill out some forms at the courthouse yourself and have a judge approve the new terms. The do-it-yourself method costs less; however, this may not be the best time to try to save a little money. Get qualified legal counsel before you agree to any adjustment of your divorce decree.

Bankruptcy

A Chapter 7 bankruptcy erases many kinds of debts, but child support and alimony are almost never included. If you are filing for bankruptcy and you owe past support, seek qualified legal help. A lawyer may not be able to have your past support amounts erased, but he may have some leeway on negotiating the time you have to pay it back.

Contest responsibility for payments

Under certain circumstances, you may not feel that you are responsible for support at all. You may not agree that the child is yours, for instance. In that case, it is not right for someone to expect you to pay money to support someone else's children, possibly even shortchanging your own. In other cases, you might not have been aware that you were creating a dependency when you had a relationship with a woman who already had children. It's better to know the rules and how to protect yourself than it is to find out the hard way.

Paternity questions

The best solution to paternity questions is to prevent them in the first place. Men need to realize that, in some ways, a liaison can have more negative results for them than for women. Yes, women are the ones who get pregnant, but men have very little control over the prevention of pregnancy, when or if they are told about the pregnancy, or whether the child is carried to term. A woman can lie and tell a man that she is on the Pill, and if a child results, he is liable for support. A man may be willing to raise a surprise baby, but a woman is free to terminate the pregnancy or, in some cases, to put the child up for adoption without his consent. It's no wonder some men feel that they have no say and no control—yet they're the ones who get stuck with the bill. Knowing what other men have gone through, it is surprising that men are willing to engage in behavior that puts them at such a risk.

Suppose a man has taken risks in the past, however. Or suppose he hasn't, but he doesn't know how to prove it. What can he do to find out if a child is really his, or prove that it isn't?

It's important to know why women name men in paternity suits. Over 80% of the paternity suits in this country are by women who are on government assistance. Many of them would rather not name their child's father, but they are in danger of losing their benefits if they do not cooperate with the agency. Depending on their lifestyle, they may not remember who could be the child's father, or there may be more than one possibility. They may not have known the child's father that well, or have any idea where he is now. To keep getting benefits, however, they are under pressure to name a father. If a woman must name the father of her child and there is some doubt as to who the father is, she is likely to name the man who has the most money, or the man she wants to be the child's father. A desperate woman may even name a man with whom she has never had a relationship, hoping to get support for her child.

Some men will readily admit paternity even if they are not sure, out of concern for the child. Few men, however, are willing to support a child that is not theirs if they do not have an ongoing relationship with the child's mother. Most men would like to know for sure whether a child is their offspring, just for peace of mind.

Fortunately, with modern blood tests, it is possible to know with a high degree of certainty if a child is yours. No longer do you have to wait to see if he looks like he has your nose or your eyes. For about $500 or less, you can take a blood test and find the answer in days. You do not even have to wait until the baby is born; some tests can now be done using a blood sample from the mother.

Blood tests are especially good at determining who cannot be a child's father. To put it simply, a child gets genes from his father and his mother. Any gene that is not from his mother must be from his father. If he has genes that cannot be accounted for by either parent, someone else must be the father. If a man takes a paternity test and the results are negative, he's free.

It's harder for a blood test to prove with certainty that someone *is* the father. A blood test may show that a man has a 90% to 99% chance of being a child's father, but that still leaves room for doubt.

Test Results

A negative paternity blood test means you are not the father. It therefore ends a paternity suit. A positive blood test, however, is only 90% to 99% accurate.

Paying for a Blood Test

If you are named in a paternity suit and you don't want to pay the cost of the blood test, you can refuse to consent to the test unless the court pays for it. If the court pays for the test and you are found to be the father, you may have to reimburse the court.

If the man lived with the child's mother or had a known relationship with her, the courts will probably decide he is the father. Otherwise, if he is still certain he is not the father, he should obtain qualified legal counsel immediately.

Custodial stepparent obligations

Stepparents may be surprised to discover that when they separate from the children's parent they are liable for support. They may have been married to the children's parent for only a short time, or they may have assumed that unless they adopted the children, the children's support was not their responsibility if the marriage broke up.

According to the law in many states, however, when a person marries someone with children, the person becomes their custodial stepparent. If the couple separates—even if the other parent packs up the kids and drives away—the stepparent must pay for their support until the divorce is final.

If you are a stepparent and separated from your spouse, seek legal counsel immediately. If a divorce is inevitable, don't delay filing for it. A finalized divorce is the best protection from claims against you as a custodial stepparent.

Many stepparents adopt their spouses' children when they marry. Adoption is forever. If you adopt your spouse's children, they are now yours as much as they are hers, and if you divorce, you will have to pay child support.

If a new stepparent adopts your children

Your obligation to provide child support ends when your children's new stepparent adopts them. Don't stop paying until you have seen final adoption paperwork, however, or you may find yourself with a past-due balance for child support.

Protecting yourself and your money

Whether you are contesting the amount you owe or not, you need to protect yourself by keeping proof of your payments. If you are contesting a substantial amount of child support or alimony payments, you may also need to take measures to make it more difficult for agencies to seize your money and other assets.

If you are disputing an amount that you owe, it may be worthwhile for you to know that child support enforcement agencies can eventually track down your employment and accounts at financial institutions. However, even in the age of computerized records, tracking down accounts takes time, and you might consider moving money to a new account every so often, until a fair agreement can be reached.

Payroll records are generally sent in once a quarter, so you usually have a little time after you get a job before the agency figures out where you are working and starts taking a cut of your pay. However, before you switch jobs just to escape the grasp of the agency, think about what constant job switching can do to your career. You are almost certainly better off staying with a steady employer, even if a large portion of your pay is deducted for support, than you will be changing jobs constantly.

Keep good records

It's not enough to make alimony and child support payments. You must make them to the right place, and you must be able to prove you made them.

For example, if you make payments to the mother of your children when you were supposed to be paying a child support collection agency, you may have to pay twice, even if the mother tells you that she is no longer on public assistance and that you should pay her directly. Always continue to pay to the agency until directed by the agency, in writing, to do otherwise.

You must also keep adequate records if you are paying alimony, because alimony is deductible on your tax return. This point cannot be overemphasized. Frequently after a divorce, the spouse or the IRS challenges the amounts the other person says he paid. Without adequate documentation, you could lose the alimony tax deduction and be ordered to pay back support if your ex-spouse makes a claim in court.

Be sure your records include:

- A list with the date and check number of each payment you send

- Original checks used for payments, if your bank returns your check (otherwise, ask your bank for copies of the payment)

- A receipt signed by your ex-spouse, if you pay in cash

Be sure to keep these records for at least three years from the date you file the tax return on which you deduct the payments.

Get help

Seek counsel from a respected legal professional if you are in a battle over child support or alimony, or if you need to contest support levels. You may be able to find low-cost legal help in your area. You can also find links to divorce and child custody laws in all fifty states and Washington, D.C., online at the FindLaw Web site at http://family.findlaw.com/divorce/divorce-alimony/state-divorce-laws .html.

16 Deal with the IRS

The bill that scares us the most

People are more intimidated by a notice from the IRS than by almost any other kind of bill. Contrary to urban legend, however, the IRS doesn't routinely storm people's houses looking for back payments and throwing the offenders in jail. The IRS wants tax payments, not bad publicity.

Even if you owe past-due taxes, you can work out a payment plan or other arrangement, depending on your situation. Unless you purposely defrauded the government, you have little to fear. The IRS may be a huge bureaucracy, and dealing with it can be undeniably frustrating at times, but most of the agency's energy is spent sending out letters, not trying to frighten citizens who make honest mistakes or who get a little behind on their taxes.

That said, don't decide you can ignore the IRS, either. They do have ways to back up those letters with more force if you don't respond. If you get notices from the IRS and you just stash them away, or toss them in the trash unopened, the IRS steps up their efforts in ways that will make you take notice.

What really happens if you get in trouble with the IRS

The consequences of tax problems depend on why you are in trouble and how you respond. What happens next also depends on how much money you owe. The IRS is practical—they won't spend as much time trying to collect $100 as they would to get $100,000.

This is what you can expect to happen in most cases:

If you don't file at all

If you don't file a return, the IRS can file one for you. This is a really bad idea, because although the IRS can usually figure out your income, they won't look for or assume any deductions. For example, if you did some side work for ABC Company for $10,000 and had $5,000 in expenses, the IRS will notice the Form 1099 that the ABC Company sent to you and the IRS, and will file a return for you and tax you on the whole $10,000. It's your job to prove that you had expenses.

If you worked as an employee, the IRS gets a copy of Form W-2 from your employer. Unless the amount is very low, they expect to see a tax return reporting that income. If they don't get one, they'll do it for you—and it won't be to your advantage.

What happens if the IRS decides you owe more money

It's no wonder we tense up when we get an envelope in the mail from the IRS. It's usually not good news. It could be a letter basically saying they don't like the way you calculated your tax return, they can't find one of your tax payments, or they have slapped on a penalty for filing late, paying late, or some other infraction.

The IRS can also do an audit of your tax returns for any or no reason, then decide you owe more money based on what they find.

Regardless of why the IRS thinks you owe more money, unless you can convince them otherwise, they begin a course of action to collect payment from you.

What happens if you don't pay the IRS when they want you to

If you owe the IRS money—or if the IRS thinks you do—you receive a series of notices. First, you get Form 501, Reminder of Unpaid

IRS lien

A lien gives the IRS legal claim to your property as security or payment for your tax debt. If the IRS tries unsuccessfully to collect past-due taxes from you, they may file a lien for the amount of your tax debt. Filing a lien notice publicly notifies your other creditors that the IRS has a claim against all your property, including property you acquire in the future.

Tax. Then, they step it up to Form 503, Urgent—Payment Required. You may get several copies of Form 503 before you get the dead serious Form 504, Final Notice.

Finally, you will receive a notice of intent to seize assets. If the IRS says that they are going to start seizing your assets, take them seriously.

The IRS has the authority to tell your bank how much money they want from your account, and to take it without telling you first. You'll get a notice in the mail telling you that the money has been seized—probably after your debit card quits working and the checks you wrote to pay your bills are all returned unpaid.

The IRS can also take your cars, garnish your wages (that is, take part of your pay), and place a lien on your home.

This all sounds like the old stories about the IRS. No wonder they still inspire such fear. What you need to know, however, is that it doesn't have to reach this point. You have to ignore a lot of letters or be highly uncooperative in most cases before the IRS resorts to such drastic measures. If you are honest and communicative, treat IRS representatives with respect, and hold up your end of the bargain with any agreement between you and the IRS, your experience with the IRS should never be this bad.

Five steps to take if the IRS says you owe them money

When you get a notice from the IRS, the way you deal with it makes a huge difference in the outcome of your situation. Follow these steps as necessary to resolve your IRS problem. If you don't understand what to do next and the amount in question is substantial, always seek professional tax help.

1. **Open and read the bill.** As with any creditor, the first rule is to never ignore the IRS. Open the envelope immediately. With any luck, it's a harmless blank form. If not, your next step depends on whether it's a notice about taxes you already knew you owed or a surprise letter.

2. **If you get a bill you didn't expect or don't understand, don't panic or rush to pay the bill.** The IRS is often wrong! It will be a lot harder to get money back after you pay it—even if you prove that the bill was wrong. Look at your returns and records and try to figure out what the problem is. If it doesn't make sense to you, and the bill is for more than a few dollars, seek professional tax advice.

3. **If the bill is wrong and you can explain the error to the IRS, write a letter stating clearly why they should remove the tax along with all penalties and interest.** For example, perhaps the IRS counted income from a Form 1099 twice. Or maybe you forgot to attach a form to your return. Send a brief, factual letter and attach copies of any proof or additional forms or schedules. Save a copy of the letter and note the date the letter is postmarked. If the IRS still thinks that you owe the money, don't give up. Keep trying to explain to them why you do not owe it. If necessary, get professional help.

4. **If you do owe the IRS money, a large portion of it may be penalties, and interest on penalties.** Before you pay, try to get the penalties reduced or removed. The IRS often reduces penalties for various reasons, especially if it means the underlying tax will be paid and they can close the case. Write a letter explaining why you think the penalty should be removed, or "abated." You must specifically ask for abatement of the penalty in your letter. Your reason could be that you made an honest mistake you are now correcting, or your bookkeeper made the mistake, or you were hospitalized. Be honest, but don't be afraid to ask for a removal of the penalty. Your debt may not look nearly as impossible to pay once the penalty is removed.

5. **File Form 9465, Installment Agreement Request, if you cannot pay the balance all at once.** If you owe more tax than you can pay by the due date, you can ask for a monthly installment agreement. The IRS *must* accept installment payments for your tax if you meet all the following requirements:

- The total amount of tax (not including penalties or interest) you owe is $25,000 or less. (The IRS may allow an installment agreement for amounts over $25,000 if you can show that you can make the payments.)

- You can show the IRS that you cannot pay the entire amount when it is due.

- You will pay off the tax within three years under the installment agreement.

- You agree to comply with the tax laws while your agreement is in effect.

- During the past five years, you (or your spouse, if filing jointly) have not failed to file or pay your taxes or had another installment agreement with the IRS.

You must pay a $43 fee, plus interest on the past-due taxes, and you may still have to pay a penalty for late payment. Pay as much as you can with your tax return to lessen the interest and penalty charges. If possible, make payments large enough that you will have the tax paid off before next year's tax return is due. The IRS can't take any collection actions on your property while your installment agreement is being considered or while the agreement is in effect. If the IRS rejects your request for an agreement, all collection activity is suspended for thirty days after the rejection and for any time during which you are appealing the rejection.

6. **If the IRS is already in collection, file an appeal to stop the collection process.** At this point, if you haven't already, you should definitely hire a tax professional to help you.

7. **If the amount you owe is more than your net worth (the total of everything you own, minus your debts), consider sending the IRS an Offer in Compromise (OIC).** An OIC is a way to negotiate your debt balance with the IRS. Use an OIC as a last resort, especially if you have a home and other assets you want to keep, because the IRS will expect your offer to at least equal your net worth. However, if you owe a huge amount of money, you may be able to settle for a fraction of the balance and be done with it.

Example: Jerry's surprise notice from the IRS

Jerry got a surprise notice from the IRS with a bill for $12,000. The bill came with very little in the way of explanation but with lots of confusing information about interest rates, penalties, and what would happen if he didn't pay. Jerry had no idea he owed the IRS anything, so a $12,000 delinquent bill was a shock. The bill said it was for failure to file a partnership return twelve years earlier. As far as Jerry knew, they had never filed late, but how could he prove it now?

Look Before You Leap

Never pay a bill from the IRS until you understand it. Even if you prove to them later that you didn't owe the money, it can take months for you to get your money back.

Getting Copies of Old Returns

If you can't find your old tax returns, you can get copies from the IRS. You can get transcripts from the IRS for free by filling out Form 4506-T, Request for Transcript of Tax Return. Transcripts may not have all attachments that were originally with your return. If you need the complete return, fill out Form 4506, Request for Copy of Tax Return. You will have to pay a fee for each return that you request. You can get both forms from the IRS Web site at http://www.irs.gov/formspubs.

Jerry's old partner, Steve, received the same bill and called Jerry in a nervous state. Steve didn't know why they owed money either, but the IRS scared him enough that he thought they should split the bill and pay it now, and argue with the IRS later.

Getting through to the IRS wasn't easy, but Jerry wasn't about to pay $12,000 without good reason. The partnership in question was a woodshop/craft operation that lasted several months and made a few hundred dollars at best. It shouldn't come back all these years later and cause so much trouble. Jerry told Steve not to pay a dime until this was settled.

Jerry called the IRS. He sat on hold, got transferred from department to department, and kept explaining his case to each new IRS representative. When he asked why, if he had filed late, he hadn't heard about it until now, one IRS representative told him that a $3,000 bill wasn't worth their time to collect, so they waited until it was $12,000 and more worthwhile. When he protested, she told him he should have filed on time in the first place.

Ironically, when Jerry tried to buy a copy of his old return from the IRS, they said they no longer had it. They don't keep returns that long. He wondered how he could be liable for a late fee for a return when no one could prove it ever existed or that it should have been filed at all. Finally, Jerry reached an IRS representative who listened to the whole story, agreed that they couldn't proceed with a case if neither party had a copy of the return in question, and moved the case into the "inactive" file.

It's important not to pay the IRS for something that doesn't make sense just because you feel intimidated. If Jerry and Steve had paid the $12,000, their chances of getting the money back would have been slim. They might have had to hire a tax attorney, which would have been expensive. It was well worth the hours spent on hold and explaining the situation over and over to different IRS representatives to solve the problem.

Protect your assets

It's not a good idea to hide assets from the IRS. Certain actions, such as lying about what you own, are a crime. If you are in the midst of a dispute, however, you might want to consider reasonable precautionary steps to protect your assets until your case is settled.

- **Rent or lease, don't buy.** The IRS can't take it if it's not yours. If you lease a car, even if you have to put money down, the IRS can't take it because it still belongs to the leasing company. The same is true of a rental home or any other item that you rent or lease.

- **Move your assets.** Don't keep all your cash in one checking account in your hometown. It will take them longer to find it if it is farther away and not all at one institution. Likewise,

keep your car either in a locked garage or at another
location—not in your driveway or nearby.

- **Give assets away.** You can transfer property titles to your children, or give collectibles to your friends. Don't get carried
away—you should only give away true gifts, not expecting to
get them back. For one thing, the recipients of your generosity
may not want to give back your gifts. If you give away large
assets, the IRS may see through the scheme and seize the assets anyway.

Avoid tax trouble in the future

Once you've been through a bout with the IRS, you'll want to avoid
any such problems in the future. You can improve your chances of
keeping on the good side of the IRS by doing the following:

- **Always file on time, even if you can't pay.** The penalties *and*
interest for filing and paying late are much higher than for
paying late alone.

- **Keep good records.** Document all your tax-related information and save your records at least seven years.

- **Stay current on each year's tax liability.** If you have tax withheld, make sure you have enough withheld to avoid surprises.
If you work as an employee and also have other taxable income, such as from self-employment, have your employer
withhold more from your paycheck to cover it. If you are self-
employed, set aside money from each check to pay your quarterly estimated tax payments. Put it in another account if
possible, and do not touch it for anything except to pay your
taxes. If your taxes are complex, or if you need help figuring
out how much to set aside for your estimated tax payments,
consult a tax professional. It will be worth it.

The IRS and You

The IRS can be frustrating to deal with. They sometimes make big mistakes and then send out a flood of paperwork before you have a chance to get the mistakes straightened out. Their phone lines are understaffed, and you can sit on hold for hours. You can't even threaten to take your business elsewhere, as you can with other creditors.

However, the IRS moves relatively slowly, and at least they give you plenty of warning before they take any serious action. They have programs and laws, such as the Taxpayer's Bill of Rights and installment agreements, in place to protect you and give you a chance to catch up on your tax bill. If you are always honest and never ignore the IRS, they can be among the most reasonable of creditors.

17 Deal with Car Payments

What if you don't make your car payments?

Many bills can be put off for a considerable amount of time before anything very serious will happen. If you don't pay your credit card bills, for example, the companies have to go through a long process of sending statements and going through collection procedures before you have to worry about anything worse than your credit report getting trashed. (Not that you'd want that to happen!) If you miss mortgage payments, the bank can start foreclosure procedures, which can take weeks or months. Even the IRS sends letter after letter before taking any drastic action.

If you miss your car payments, however, it's a different matter. Your car loan is attached to your car, just the way your home mortgage is attached to your house. Unlike a house, however, a car is not protected by tenant eviction laws. Lenders can move very quickly to declare you in default and repossess your car.

Technically, if you are one day late on your car payment, you are in default on your loan and the lender can take your car away. Even if you are never late on a payment, the lender can choose to declare you to be in default on your loan if, for example, you let your insurance lapse, you damage the car significantly, or you refuse to let the lender examine the car.

Most lenders are not that eager to take your car, fortunately.

They would much rather finish what they started and collect your payments—especially if they will have a hard time getting as much money out of your car as you owe on the loan. They may even give you some flexibility in your payments if you ask for it, and you usually have some time, at least a few months, to make good on your past-due car payments before they actually seize your car.

What to do if you're having trouble making your car payments

If you are having trouble making your car payments, the sooner you do something about it, the more options you have. Basically, you have four options:

1. Keep making your car payments by adjusting your other priorities or earning more money.

2. Ask for a temporary reprieve from full payments or a rescheduling of payments.

3. Find a loan with a lower interest rate and refinance.

4. Get rid of your car.

Doing nothing is not an option. If you do nothing, your car will certainly be repossessed. You will lose your car and everything you have put into it so far, and a repossession due to nonpayment will show up on your credit record.

A Chapter 7 bankruptcy isn't a very good option. It can't get you out of car payment debt, because the debt is secured by the car. Unless you have a lot of other debts, filing for bankruptcy won't help you. If you do file for bankruptcy and you owe money on a car, you are usually allowed to keep making payments on your car loan after the bankruptcy. Nothing much changes—you keep the car, but you also keep making the payments. When you file for a Chapter 7 bankruptcy, you also have the option of voluntarily giving up the car and not making more car payments or owing any deficiency balance. If your loan balance is a lot lower than the value of the car, however, you may have significant equity in the car. (Equity equals the car's value minus what you still owe on it.) In that case, the bankruptcy trustee may require you to sell the car so he can use the equity to pay your other creditors.

Here are your four viable options in more detail:

1. **Keep making your payments by adjusting your priorities or earning more money.** In chapter 3, you created a budget with the amounts you are currently earning and spending each month. In chapter 12, you worked on budget goals, deciding how much you choose to earn and spend each month. If you are still working on your goal budget and you want to keep your car, see what expense categories you can cut back on to have enough money to afford your car payments. After all, if you need your car to get to work, it's worth scrimping on some other budget categories to save your transportation. Perhaps you'd rather work more so you can keep your car. Calculate how much weekend work, overtime, or other work you would have to do to make your car payments. Sometimes a combination of working a bit more and spending less can make seemingly impossible car payments suddenly seem within reach.

2. **Ask for a temporary reprieve from full payments.** As soon as you know that you will miss a full payment, contact the finance company. There may be a grace period for late payment. If you expect to be able to make your payment shortly—for example, if you are receiving a paycheck the following week—they may put a note in your file that you called and take no action unless you don't follow through. The company may even waive any late fee, especially if you have made your payments faithfully up to this point. If you won't be able to make full car payments for some time—for exam-

ple, if you are seriously ill and missing weeks or months of work—see if the finance company will work with you. You may be able to negotiate a temporary reprieve from payments, during which interest will continue to be added to your balance, or a revised payment schedule, stretching it out longer and lowering the monthly amount. As always, get any change to the contract in writing.

3. **Find a loan with a lower interest rate.** Car loans are not always the best deals, in part because people often don't shop around for them. They take the most convenient financing— usually the one offered at the dealership. There's nothing to stop you, however, from finding a better loan deal anytime in the life of the car. Your bank or credit union may offer a competitive rate to refinance your car, or you may get a better rate by using a home equity line of credit. A lower rate, possibly with an extended schedule, may reduce your car payments to a level you can handle. It's probably not a good idea to pay off your car loan with a lower-interest credit card or any other loan that is not guaranteed to maintain an interest rate below a certain level. You could find yourself paying more than before.

4. **Get rid of your car.** A creditor may refuse to accept late payments or make any other concessions and may demand you return the car. If you cannot keep your car, it is better to voluntarily return it than it is to "make them come get it." If they are forced to repossess the car, their expenses will be higher, and if they do not recoup all their costs, you will have to pay the difference. If you sell your car yourself, you may have cash left over after you pay off your car loan, or you may at least owe the car finance company less than if they take the car and auction it off wholesale. You will generally get the most money by selling to a private party yourself rather than taking the car to a dealership; you might try placing a

newspaper ad, putting a notice on local and work bulletin boards, or sticking a sign in the car window.

Delay repossession of your car while you work on other solutions

If your car may be repossessed, you need to find out what your specific rights are and how much time you have while you work on other long-term solutions. Your rights and the amount of time you have depend on the laws of your state and the terms of your financing contract. Some states protect consumers and give them more opportunity than other states to catch up on payments or even to redeem their own car after it is repossessed. A few states require companies to get a court order before they can repossess a car. Other states allow financing companies to repossess cars without notifying their owners first.

Most states offer consumers some protection by not allowing companies to "breach the peace" when they repossess a car. This means that collectors can't break into your garage, or take your car from your driveway if you or one of your relatives tries to stop them. Nor can they use verbal or physical intimidation. They can, however, tell you lies or trick you into letting them take the car. The less you tell anyone who comes to your home or workplace looking for your car, the better.

You can delay repossession by keeping your car in a locked garage or at another location. Don't try just parking your car two or three blocks away on the street, however. Repossession companies are wise to that, and they will find it.

Eventually, even if you hide your car or keep it locked in your garage, the finance company can get a court order, and you will have to give up your car or be in contempt of court.

CAUTION: If you think your car may be repossessed, don't leave any valuables in it, such as personal items, stereos, or CDs. The finance company may not be allowed to keep or sell your personal property, but it may take you some trouble to get it back. If a stereo is installed, it may be considered part of the car and be sold with it, even if you installed the stereo after you financed the car.

Watch out for deficiency balances!

Many people think that once the finance company has come and taken the car, it's over. They discover later that even though they don't have a car, they still owe money to the finance company. This happens if the amount the company gets out of the car is less than the total of what you still owed on the loan plus the expenses of repossession and sale. The financing company sues you for the difference.

You have no control over how much the company spends repossessing and selling the car or how cheaply the company sells it at an auction. This is one reason you should explore all other options, including selling the car yourself, before you allow a car to be repossessed.

Decide if your car is worth it

One of the most common money mistakes people make is spending too much on their vehicle. By the time they make their car payments and pay for insurance, gas, and upkeep, they may be spending half their income on transportation. All too often, they aren't even aware how much their car is costing them, or how they could get around just as comfortably for less.

Carol came to me for help with her budget. She was starting a new dog-grooming business and needed a budget to show the bank when she applied for a loan. She drove up in a nice new sedan—pretty impressive for a young woman about to start a business. As we worked on her budget, however, one expense item stood out from all the others: her car. All her other expenses were fairly low, but she was paying way more than she could afford for transportation.

Help! I Can't Pay My Bills

Carol had a hard time accepting the fact that she couldn't afford her car. She was used to driving a nice car. What would people think if she started driving an older, smaller car? Besides, she had put almost nothing down when she bought the car, so she owed considerably more on it now than it was worth. That's the catch with buying a new car: The car's value goes down rapidly the first year or two that you own it, much faster than you can pay off the loan. Between her pride and her negative equity in the car, she didn't see how she could sell it. She felt trapped.

What can you do if you find yourself paying for more car than you can afford? First, look at your options. This Transportation Cost Comparison worksheet shows the amount one person is spending on her car every month now, and three ways that she can try to save money.

Transportation Cost Comparison

Date _____

Use this worksheet to compare up to four transportation options. The sample options are:
* Current Car. Continuing to drive your car everywhere, including to work and back.
* Higher MPG Car. Buying a car that gets better gas mileage.
* Current Car and Bus. Taking the bus to work and driving your car the rest of the time.
* Bus and Taxis. Doing without a car by taking the bus to work and taking occasional taxis.

	Current Car	Higher MPG Car	Current Car and Bus	Bus and Taxis
Miles per Gallon (MPG)	20	30	20	n/a
Monthly commuting miles using car	600	600	0	0
Monthly other miles using car	400	400	400	0
Price of gas per gallon	3	3	3	n/a
FIXED TRANSPORTATION EXPENSES - Expenses that generally stay the same				
2 Car insurance	180	200	150	
3 Car payments	400	500	400	
4 One-month bus pass	0	0	70	70
5				
6				
7				
8				
9				
VARIABLE EXPENSES - Expenses that vary from month to month				
15 Car maintenance	50	50	40	0
16 Taxis, $40, 8 times per month	0	0	0	320
17 Gas (Miles driven X Price of gas per gallon/MPG)	150	100	60	0
18 Oil	10	10	10	0
19 Car washes	10	10	10	0
20				
21				
22				
TOTAL EXPENSES	800	870	740	390

The first thing people often think of is to buy a car that gets better gas mileage. In this example, the first column shows one person's current transportation expenses. The second column, Higher MPG Car, shows total monthly transportation costs with a newer car that gets more miles per gallon of gas. Unfortunately, the higher car payment and insurance more than cancels out the savings in gasoline. This is usually the case. Unless you can buy a car for something close to the value of the one you have now, buying a different car to save on gas doesn't usually pay off. In states that charge a sales tax on the resale of vehicles, the tax alone wipes out any savings on gasoline for a long time to come.

Column 3, Current Car and Bus, shows the option of keeping the current car and taking the bus to work. Most people don't realize how much it costs them to drive a car. The gasoline is only the beginning. Service, maintenance, insurance, and wear and tear on your car are expensive over the long haul. In this example, the person can save a substantial amount of money by taking the bus to work every day; $60 a month is $720 a year—not pocket change!

In the last column, Bus and Taxis, you can see what it would cost this person if she sells her car and takes the bus most of the time. When a bus won't take her where she wants to go, she'll call a taxi. A combination of taking buses and hiring taxis is much cheaper than owning and maintaining a car. It may be inconvenient at times, especially if you don't live in an area with great public transportation, but it is possible.

Use this blank Transportation Cost Comparison worksheet to figure out your own options, or download it online at *HelpICant PayMyBills.net*.

The no-car-payment plan

If you only learn one thing from this book, learn this: If you can get along without car payments, do it. Very few things will so profoundly

Help! I Can't Pay My Bills

Transportation Cost Comparison

Use this worksheet to compare up to four transportation options. The sample options are:
* Current Car. Continuing to drive your car everywhere, including to work and back.
* Higher MPG Car. Buying a car that gets better gas mileage.
* Current Car and Bus. Taking the bus to work and driving your car the rest of the time.
* Bus and Taxis. Doing without a car by taking the bus to work and taking occasional taxis.

		Current Car	Higher MPG Car	Current Car and Bus	Bus and Taxis
	Miles per Gallon (MPG)				
	Monthly commuting miles using car				
	Monthly other miles using car				
	Price of gas per gallon				
	FIXED TRANSPORTATION EXPENSES - Expenses that generally stay the same				
2	Car insurance				
3	Car payments				
4	One-month bus pass				
5					
6					
7					
8					
9					
	VARIABLE EXPENSES - Expenses that vary from month to month				
15	Car maintenance				
16	Taxis, $40, 8 times per month				
17	Gas (Miles driven X Price of gas per gallon/MPG)				
18	Oil				
19	Car washes				
20					
21					
22					
	TOTAL EXPENSES				

affect your financial future as whether or not you have to make car payments.

If you can, buy a car that you can afford to pay for with cash. Otherwise, buy the cheapest car that will get you to work and back, and pay your car loan off as quickly as possible. Then, take the money you're not spending on car payments and start saving for your next car. This strategy of always saving for the next car, instead

Overheard

"Only poor people buy new cars."—*well-to-do businessman on plane* of paying for the one you're driving, can make an incredible difference in how comfortably you live the rest of your life.

Make it your goal to never have car payments again

Ken and Val's VW Rabbit was falling apart. The side window fell out, the inside door handle fell off. With Baby #2 in his car seat, they wanted a bigger, nicer car. As they filled out the paperwork for a new car loan, Val asked offhandedly, "How much more would the payment be if we paid it off in three years?"

It turned out that the payments for a three-year loan weren't much higher than they would be on a four-year loan, so Ken and Val thought that sounded like a good idea. Three years later, they had a party to celebrate their last car payment. Not having car payments was like getting a raise! They thought, "Wouldn't it be great if we never had a car payment again?"

If signing up for a three-year loan was Ken and Val's first smart move, keeping their car a long time was their second. By the time that car was seven years old, they had saved enough money to buy the next car with cash.

That's when they discovered another advantage of paying cash: It's a lot easier to stick to a predetermined price when you only have so much cash in the kitty. The salesman can talk all he wants and tell you how another few thousand dollars won't make much difference in your monthly payments, but when you tell him you only have this much cash and you're not taking out a loan, he won't get far. In Ken and Val's case, the salesman was persistent. They told him that they had $13,000 and not a dollar more—which was true. He agreed to sell them a car for that, but then he kept finding a fee here and an extra option there. "No," Ken said, "we're writing a check for no more than $13,000." The salesman gave in on everything but the floor mats. He was determined to charge extra for them—so Ken and Val drove away without floor mats. They never missed them.

That was two cars ago, but Ken and Val haven't had car payments since. Although their income has fluctuated over the years, they have always lived comfortably. They attribute their success not only to staying out of credit card debt but also to never again having car payments. They especially appreciated the freedom from debt a few years ago, when they were unemployed for a time. They were able to cut their expenses and get by on very little until Ken found another job in California. If they had had to make payments on one or two cars, the time off work would have been much more stressful!

In most parts of the country, driving a car is a big part of our lives. With some planning ahead, we can enjoy the freedom that driving a car gives us, without letting car expenses take a disproportionate amount of our income.

18

Deal with Credit Card Bills

*Reduce, negotiate, and pay off
your plastic debts*

You've spent the money—you owe the money. Or do you? If you look at your credit card balance and say, "I can't possibly have spent that much," chances are you didn't. A large share of what you owe may be interest, penalties, and fees for who-knows-what. These charges can pile up alarmingly fast until you have such a mountain of debt that you don't know how you'll ever pay it off. Take Lee, for example.

Lee got a new credit card with a $1,200 limit. He promptly spent the $1,200, which was easy because most of his income goes to pay his mortgage and his other credit card payments. He didn't spend any more on the card after that. Lee admits he might have missed a payment or two, and he may not have opened every envelope and noticed as the interest rate went from 18% to 25% and then to over 33%. Once the fees caused his balance to go over the $1,200 limit, he started getting overlimit fees, as well. Last time he dared look, he owed over $7,000, and the credit card company was demanding $1,800 immediately. Lee has a good job with the school district, but he doesn't make enough money to afford payments like that.

Lee was astounded at the fees and the interest rate hikes. He asked, "Can they do that?" Yes, they can. Lee thought that when he spent the original $1,200 on a card with 18% interest he had basically signed up for an 18% loan. Unfortunately, nothing in his credit card agreement said the rate was fixed. If he had wanted a fixed-rate loan, he should have gotten one at the bank. Unless the agreement says otherwise, an interest rate on a credit card can change for any or no reason. When Lee spent more than he could pay off immediately, he put himself at risk. When he missed "a payment or two," he was headed for disaster.

How much of your balance is from things you bought?

Have you ever wondered why there's nothing on your credit card statement that tells you how much of your total balance is actually from your purchases? Sure, it tells you how much of this month's new charges are from purchases. But what about the balance you carry forward—how much is from purchases, and how much is from interest and charges, and interest and charges on prior interest and charges? If you carry a balance forward for very many months, chances are a large portion of your balance is not from things you have bought but from other charges.

The question now is, do you really owe all that money? Legally, yes. Ethically, it's arguable. As a practical matter, possibly not. Credit card companies often use their discretion to reduce interest and fees when it is to their advantage. You may find them to be more willing to negotiate the amount you owe than you thought.

Credit card companies make most of their money when you buy things using their card and then pay for your purchases over time, along with interest charges. (The credit card companies also generally receive a percentage of every purchase you make on your card directly from the merchants, so they make money even if you never pay interest.) They want to keep you happy so you'll keep using their card and making payments. They don't want you to switch cards, stop making payments altogether, or go bankrupt. Because they want to keep you as a paying customer, you have a considerable amount of clout.

Ask them to reduce your balance

Asking the credit card company to simply reduce the amount you owe them may sound crazy, but that's exactly what you can do if you have a good reason. You may be able to have current fees reversed, and if your situation warrants, you may be able to negotiate a lower total balance.

Reverse current fees

Every month when you get your credit card statement, immediately open it and check for interest fees, late fees, overlimit fees, and other charges. Don't put it off. It's a lot easier to get fees reversed when they are fresh, and you want to reverse them before you pay interest and late fees on the charges themselves.

Most people don't know that if they usually pay their bills on time but once in a while slip up and get their payment in a few days late, companies will almost always take the late fee off when asked. I went on vacation a couple of months ago, and by the time I came back and paid my bills, I was two days late on a department store bill. I got slapped with a $30 late fee on a $72 balance. "Of all the nerve!" I thought, as I considered ceremoniously melting my card over the nearest candle and never shopping in their store again. I like that store, though, so I contained myself long enough to call the customer service number on my statement. I told the representative that I was two days late and got a $30 late fee. Before I could make a fool of myself ranting on and threatening to cancel my card, she said that she'd reverse the fee. Just like that.

I should have known they would reverse the charges. Over the years, I have called different banks and card companies numerous times about late fees and other charges, and I have always gotten a positive response. Never once have they said, "I see, this is the first time you've been late, but that's too bad! Two days late is two days late!" They have always reduced or completely taken off the extra fees. They even removed the interest once when my online bill payment for the entire balance got there right after the grace period ended.

This tactic may not work so well if I start paying late every month and asking for forgiveness of late fees and interest every time. Respect is a two-way street, and if I want to be treated like a valuable customer, I have to act like one.

Finding out if you can have fees removed from your current bill is easy. Pick up the phone and call the toll-free number on your credit card statement. Explain your situation politely and matter-of-factly. If they don't suggest removing the fee, suggest it yourself. If they still don't think so, and you mean it, tell them you may cancel your card. Point out how long you've been a loyal customer. You might be able to save $30 or more with a two-minute phone call. It doesn't hurt to ask.

Negotiate the entire balance

If you are in deep financial trouble but you are serious about making good on your debts, credit card companies are usually willing to work with you. They are not likely to accept less than the amount they have paid merchants on your behalf—the money you have actually spent—but they do have room to negotiate the amount that is due to interest and fees. You can ask them to drastically reduce the total amount you owe them, with the implied or stated alternative that otherwise you may not be able to pay at all, or that you may be forced into bankruptcy. Balance negotiation is not something you want to try unless you really need to, and for obvious reasons you won't want to try it repeatedly. Be aware, also, that your credit report will show that you negotiated your balance.

Balance negotiation is a little more involved than calling to get a one-time fee reversed. You'll want to write a letter and keep a copy for your records. The letter does not have to be long; in, fact it should be direct and to the point. It should include:

- Your name and account number

- Brief history; i.e., how long you have had the account, how long you have been a customer in good standing, and how much you owe

- Why you need to negotiate the balance

- What you are suggesting

- If applicable, what may happen if you are unable to negotiate (don't mention bankruptcy unless you mean it—even mentioning bankruptcy may be noted on your credit file)

Send your letter to the customer service department. If you don't receive a response within thirty days, follow up with a phone call or another letter.

Sample Letter to Credit Card Company

Customer Service Department
National Bank
123 Main Street
Big City, NY 12345
June 1, 2007

Re: Sue and Vern Ashlock
Account # 1234567

We have had a credit card with National Bank since 1999. Up until December of 2006, we made our payments regularly and on time. Our current balance is $15,235.56, and our minimum monthly payment is $533.

In December, Sue lost her job at ABC Hospital. Sue's job had provided our main source of income. She is receiving unemployment benefits. However, on our reduced income we have not been able to keep up with mounting debts. Even if Sue finds a comparable job soon, we are in a financially untenable position unless we can work something out with our creditors.

If you are willing to accept $7,618, or 50% of the current balance, we would like to make good on the reduced balance. With minimum monthly payments of under $300, we expect to be able to keep up with our payments and, when Sue returns to work, make progress paying off the balance.

Thank you for your understanding and help.

Sincerely,
Sue and Vern Ashlock
808-111-2222

Minimize future interest charges and fees

Now that you realize how much of your debt is from interest charges and fees, you understand how important it is to minimize them from now on. No matter how hard you try to save money, it won't do much good if you are constantly getting hit with high interest rates and all kinds of unnecessary fees.

Avoid late payment fees

Remember when we used to have thirty days to pay most bills? Most bills were due around the same time of the month anyway, so we could pay our bills once a month and then forget it until next month. That's not the way it is now. I get bills that are due twenty days from the statement date, and it took them ten days to get to me. That gives me ten days to pay them, which pretty much assumes I get my mail, open it, and sit down and pay the bills. It's not just my cards, either: Consumer advocates have noticed that the amount of time people are given to pay their bills has been steadily shrinking. By no coincidence, the amount the credit card companies are collecting in late fees is rising.

Your first defense against late fees is to keep track of when every bill is due. That way, even if a bill gets lost, you will know when it needs to be paid. You can always send something, even if you don't have the bill, or you can call the credit card company and find out what the balance is.

One way to keep track of bill due dates is to make a simple list on a computer spreadsheet of all your bills and the day each bill is due. If you sort the list by date, you can easily refer to the list throughout the month to make sure every bill is paid on time.

If you don't want to use a spreadsheet, you can do the same thing on paper. Sort the stack of bills by the day of the month they are due, and then handwrite the list. Post it by your desk or other bill-paying center so you can keep an eye on it.

Another tactic is to use a computerized reminder system. If you use personal finance software, such as MSN Money or Quicken, you can set up your software to remind you when payments are due. You can even have your computer's calendar remind you; I set reminders on Microsoft Outlook, and it works fine.

If you usually keep enough in your checking account to cover small withdrawals, you can also use another tactic to avoid late fees: automatic payments. I don't like to set up automatic payments for large bills or for bills that are not the same every month—I need to keep tabs on things a little better than that—but I have small minimum monthly payments sent automatically to my credit card companies via online bill pay. When I get the monthly statement, I pay the balance minus the automatic payment. When I'm late, which happens occasionally despite my best efforts, the small automatic payment saves me from any late fees or embarrassment.

Prevent overlimit fees

Overlimit fees can be a nasty surprise. Often these fees seem high, especially if you've been making your payments faithfully and your only crime is purchasing too much within one monthly cycle. You don't even have to spend more than the limit. As Lee discovered in our earlier example, interest charges and fees can bump your previously acceptable balance over the limit—and then add a second injury to the first with an overlimit fee.

There's only one solution to overlimit fees. You must know your credit limits, and you must avoid them the way you would the edge of a cliff. If your credit limit is $3,000 on a card, try to keep it under $2,000—or less if you share the card with someone else. Most banks now make balance information available online. Go ahead and register so you can check your balance quickly and frequently, especially before you charge those airline tickets. You may also be able to use an automated phone system that tells you your balance anytime, without even having to talk to a representative.

If you are getting close to a credit limit, call and request an increase. If you are in good standing, you will usually get it. It's amazing the difference a phone call can make. If you call before you make a charge, the company may cheerfully raise your limit. If you charge over the limit without calling first, you may get a curt letter informing you of your transgression, and an extra fee to boot!

Choose cards with no annual fees

Annual fees are almost never necessary these days. So many banks are vying for your business that it's hard to see why you should have to pay an annual fee just to have a card. If you have a card that carries an annual fee, you stand a good chance of having the fee removed—even if it's already on your statement—if you call and ask. If the representative doesn't want to remove the fee, don't give up too quickly. You may have to talk to a supervisor, or you may have to switch to another one of the company's plans, but chances are you can get rid of the fee. If not, consider shopping for another company's card.

A card with an annual fee may be worth it, however, if it makes up for it in other ways. If I carried a large balance on a card, I'd rather pay an annual $50 fee on a card with 10% interest than use a card with no fee and pay 18% interest. I do have one card with an annual fee, but I don't feel bad about the $50 a year because I get free hotel rooms every so often based on what I spend. That card makes it well worth it.

Minimize interest charges

Americans spend huge amounts of money on interest charges. Yet they often seem unaware of how much they are paying, or whether they are getting the best deal. They take the most convenient financing, like in-house financing at the furniture store, rather than shop around. They sign up for credit cards because an offer came in their mailbox—instead of searching *Bankrate.com* or other online sites to find a card with a lower rate. They don't even always notice when their credit card rates go up; they sometimes assume they are still paying the rate they signed up for, when in fact it may be twice as high by now.

The key to minimizing your interest charges is always being fully aware of how much you are paying. When you know what interest is costing you, you can take steps to minimize your interest charges. If you lower your interest expense, you can apply more of your money to your balances and eventually eliminate credit card interest altogether.

First, look at the Debts worksheet you filled out in chapter 3. In the Interest Rate column, you can see the rate you are paying on each of your debts. Plan to eliminate your debts, one by one, starting with the debts with the highest interest rate.

If you are barely able to make the minimum payments on your

debt, being told to pay off your debts to save on interest charges may sound unrealistic. "Sure," you think, "if I could pay them off I wouldn't be in this fix!" The fact is, there is seldom a case where something can't be done to lower fees or otherwise find cash that you can apply to the balance to start reducing your debt load.

For example, say you look at your Debt worksheet and see that you have five credit cards, with interest rates varying from 9% to 21%. The 21% rate is killing you. Your top priority is to stop paying such an unconscionable rate. Unless you do something, you will be in debt bondage for years. You have three options:

1. Ask the company with the 21% rate to lower the rate.

2. Ask for a higher credit limit (if necessary) on your 9% card, so you can transfer your balance from the higher-interest card to the lower-interest card.

3. Get a new card or loan with a lower interest rate, and use it to pay off the high-interest card.

Of the three options, the first one is the easiest and most preferable. You can make one phone call and possibly lower your interest rate significantly, especially if the interest rate is higher than rates on other cards. Why open more credit card accounts if you can keep the old one with a lower rate? The company is probably offering new customers lower rates right now to entice them to sign up; don't you think it would lower your rate to keep you signed up? Besides, your credit rating can suffer if you are constantly applying for new cards. Give your old credit card company a chance first.

If you have cards with lower rates, and you have available credit on them, by all means transfer your balance. Don't charge any more on your high-interest cards—don't even carry them around in your wallet. If you must use a credit card, stick to your lower-interest ones.

If the company won't lower the interest rate on your card and you can't transfer your debt to a card with a lower rate, you may need to get another card or some other loan. You can choose from thousands of credit cards available all over the country, or you may need to get a home equity loan or a personal loan. For more information about borrowing to get through tough times, see chapter 8.

Once you have a lower interest rate, your minimum payment will be smaller. The important thing now, if it is at all possible, is to keep paying the amount that you would have paid at the old interest rate. The amount you save with the new, lower interest rate will now go to reduce the amount you owe, and you will start to make progress on paying off your debt. It's a great deal all around: By reducing your interest charges you can start paying your way out of debt without paying a dime more than you were before.

If you can come up with enough money to make larger payments on your debt, so much the better! By following some of the other strategies in this book, from cutting optional services to watching your budget and adjusting your income tax withholding, you may be able to find money to apply to your debt. As your balance goes down, your minimum payments will generally go down, too. Whenever possible, pay more than the minimum amount.

Update your Debts worksheet periodically to see how you're doing. Watching your high-interest credit cards disappear and your total debt balance shrink is very rewarding and motivating. Keep working on the debts with the highest interest rates, and you can wipe them out faster than you ever thought possible.

19 Make Your Mortgage Payment

Don't let foreclosure steal your home, your equity, and your credit rating

If you find yourself behind in your mortgage payments, it might sound like a good idea to "let the bank take it back." That's a move you will probably regret. As discussed in chapter 4, letting the bank take your home back—in other words, enduring foreclosure—can leave you with no place to live, no equity from your home, and bad credit. You may still owe money when it's over, and you may owe tax on any amount the bank forgives or can't collect.

Take my House, Please

A few people have the misconception that the option of giving their house to the bank is part of the mortgage agreement. All they have to do is quit making payments, and the bank gets the house—no hard feelings. In fact, the bank doesn't want their house. Banks are not generally in the real estate business. They are in the business of loaning money and collecting payments in return, which is what people agree to when they sign up for a mortgage.

You have more options than ever, though. With some planning, you should be able to keep your house or at least sell it for a fair price. You may be able to sell your house and still live in it, or retain the right to buy it back in the future. Even if you have waited so long that foreclosure is imminent, you can still make the best of the situation.

How to keep your house

If you haven't missed a payment yet, or if you can possibly catch up, the best thing you can do is to put your mortgage at the top of your list every month and keep it current. Even if you fall behind in credit card payments and other bills, always pay your mortgage. For one thing, shelter is next to food in the hierarchy of needs. You need a place to live. For another thing, your home is your biggest investment. For many people, when they reach retirement age, their home is their only real investment, other than Social Security. Don't throw it away lightly. Finally, if you are ever forced into bankruptcy, you can probably keep your home. (Check on the laws in your state.) That's called a home exemption. You lose that exemption if you have already lost your home.

If you are further behind, or if you don't see how you will be able to make your full payments in the near future, you need to contact your bank immediately. Don't send partial payments without contacting them first, and don't just drop out of sight.

Being short of money is embarrassing, and the last thing you want to do is to call them. But you are in a far better position if you call them than if you wait for them to call you. Many banks regularly make provisions for people who are unemployed or sick and who need to work out an alternate plan for the time being. You may be surprised at how willing they are to work with you. They want to keep you as a customer, and they really, really don't want to foreclose. Call them.

If your loan is insured by the government

If you have a government-insured loan, such as an FHA or a VA loan, you may qualify for other exceptions and assistance. For more information about foreclosure prevention on an FHA loan, see the U.S. Department of Housing and Urban Development Web site at http://www.hud.gov/foreclosure/index.cfm. For information about preventing foreclosure on a VA loan, contact the U.S. Department of Veterans Affairs (http://www.homeloans.va.gov).

Use innovative arrangements to avoid foreclosure

One way to avoid foreclosure is to find an investor that will agree to an arrangement that benefits both of you. You'll generally have to find a private investor, but if you find one that is honest and is willing to share the risk and profits with you, you can both win.

In one such scenario that has been used successfully in Oregon, the investor buys the house and gives the homeowner a lease option to buy the house back sometime in the future. Generally, the investor and the homeowner split the homeowner's current equity. The simplest way to do this is to sell the house to the investor for slightly more than the mortgage amount, and include a lease option that gives you, the (former) homeowner, the right to lease the house for a stated period of years and then buy it back if you want to at the end of the lease period. If you are in an area where home prices are rising, you can also offer the investor a portion of the amount the home goes up in value during the lease period. Be sure to include a limit on this amount, or you may find yourself priced out of your house when you get ready to exercise your option to buy it back.

Don't agree to lease payments for more than you can realistically pay, or you may still lose your home and your place to live.

As always, get the agreement in writing and have a lawyer read it before you sign anything.

*Use a reverse mortgage to save your home
and get monthly income*

If you have owned your home for a long time, or if you made a sizable down payment when you bought it, you may have a significant equity in your home. Going through foreclosure and losing that equity would be a terrible loss. One way to tap the equity in your home is by using a reverse mortgage.

A reverse mortgage is the opposite of a regular mortgage. With a regular mortgage, you make payments on the mortgage until it is paid off. Then, the house is yours, free and clear. With a reverse mortgage, you get paid a lump sum or monthly payment. Each payment your receive reduces your equity in your home.

If you sell your home in a few years, the debt you owe on the reverse mortgage reduces the amount you receive from the sale, just like any other mortgage. If you don't sell, but you use up all the equity in your home, your mortgage contract may allow you to stay in your home if you pay real estate taxes and insurance premiums.

Most applicants for reverse mortgages are retired. They figure they need their home for a limited number of remaining years, so they don't mind chipping away at their equity in return for receiving cash now. If you have enough equity, you should be able to qualify for a reverse mortgage even if you are retired and can't show a substantial income. Since you'll be receiving money, not paying it, your income doesn't affect whether you qualify for the loan.

Don't enter into a reverse mortgage lightly. One of the biggest drawbacks to a reverse mortgage is the up-front cost. You may be charged $5,000 or more up front to get the mortgage, and then you will pay a monthly service fee. For this reason, you shouldn't take out a reverse mortgage if you may sell your home in just a few years. You're better off selling the home to get your equity and saving the service fees.

You should also skip a reverse mortgage if you want to pass your home down to your children when you die. It may be difficult or impossible for them to inherit a house that comes encumbered by a large mortgage. If you receive most of the equity in your home over time, when you die, the house will probably be sold to pay the mortgage.

Under the right circumstances, a reverse mortgage can provide you with what otherwise may seem impossible: the security of staying in your own home plus cash in your pocket.

If you decide that you can't keep your house

If the bank has already started foreclosure proceedings and you absolutely don't see any way to save your house, some experts recommend not trying to make any more payments. Their reasoning is that you're going to lose the house anyway, and making additional payments at this point is sending money to a lost cause. Instead, they say to save your money so you can afford to get into another place. This makes some sense if you think you have no other options.

Before you resign yourself to losing your house through foreclosure, however, look at those other options. Communicate with the bank. Explain your situation, and ask for suggestions.

Sometimes they will let you deed the house back to them in lieu of foreclosure. This prevents you from getting the black mark of foreclosure on your credit report, although a deed in lieu of foreclosure may be recorded instead. It is much less expensive for the bank— which matters to you if you live in one of the states where you could still owe them money if they don't recoup what you owe them from the sale of your home. Ask a legal professional in your state or seek free legal counsel if this rule may apply to you.

Remember, if you deed the house back to the bank, you won't get any money from the sale of the house, no matter how much equity you had in it. If you are offering to deed the house to the bank, try to negotiate with them. Ask them to refrain from putting negative information on your credit report, and ask for more time to look for another place before you have to move.

Sometimes the bank will agree to rent your house back to you, at least for a limited time, after you deed it to them. This helps them because they have an income stream until the house is sold. Ask for at least a three-month or six-month lease, and expect to pay no more than 50% to 75% of your former mortgage payment. After all, you're not getting tax deductions for the interest and property tax payments anymore, and you're not building up equity.

If you have any time left before foreclosure is final, and no other options left, try to sell your home. You won't have your home to live in anymore, but you will avoid having foreclosure on your credit record, and you may receive some badly needed cash from the sale.

Sell your home for a fair price

If your home is in danger of foreclosure, now is not the time to take half-measures in your attempt to sell it. In ordinary times, you might be able to save thousands of dollars by selling your home yourself. When you are in danger of losing everything, it's time to find an expert! You probably need a real estate agent—and not just any agent, or the agent who charges the least money. You need an experienced agent who takes his or her profession seriously. It helps if he has great contacts and is very familiar with your local area.

Finding the best real estate agent is not as easy as walking into the nearest real estate office or choosing one who looks reasonably smart based on his picture in the glossy ads. In my opinion, it is harder to find a good real estate agent than an expert in most other professional fields, for several reasons:

- Entry to the real estate field is relatively easy compared to other fields. Yes, they must study and pass tests, but getting a basic real estate license takes weeks, not years. This ease of entry encourages many people to try real estate sales who may not understand the skills and commitment required to become a top-notch professional.

- Turnover in the real estate industry is high. Many new real estate agents never make it past the first year, and about 55% of the agents in the average real estate firm leave, either for another firm or another profession, every year.

- Many people who call themselves real estate agents are, frankly, investors. They are more interested in finding good deals for themselves and their friends than they are in earning commissions. I called one once and told him I was looking for investment properties, specifically for a good deal on property that possibly needed minor upgrades. He told me if he found anything like that, he or the other agents would buy it themselves. Another time, I made a bid on a house, only to be outbid by the listing co-agent. Since then, I always ask real estate agents if they are in the business of selling real estate or if they are mostly just looking for deals themselves.

So how do you find a good real estate agent? The best way to get started is to get a referral from someone who had a successful experience with one. You might also find someone by going to open houses and talking to real estate agents there, or by going to a real estate office in your local area and asking to speak to an experienced listing agent. Don't be charmed too quickly, however. Before you sign anything, ask these questions:

- How long has this person been selling real estate?

- How many hours a week does he spend on real estate? Does he have another job or business in addition to real estate sales?

- How does his sales record compare to that of other agents in the area?

- What hours is he available? When is he not available?

- How will he promote this house?

You can't afford to take a chance with an inexperienced agent when you are in a hurry to sell. Find the smartest, most experienced, and most professional agent in your area. Ask for his advice, and take it. He will be worth every penny of his commission if he helps you get a fair price for your house as quickly as possible.

Watch out for unscrupulous investors and foreclosure vultures

People go to seminars and take courses on how to buy houses fast and cheap from desperate people. If you go to an online bookstore such as Amazon.com and type "foreclosure" as the search keyword, most of the books that come up will be not about avoiding foreclosure but about buying real estate at or immediately before foreclosure. As these books point out, even if the buyers only pay the amount owed on the mortgage, they keep the stigma of foreclosure off the sellers' credit record and get them off the hook. They may even pay a few thousand extra—enough to help the sellers move and get into an apartment.

One thing that foreclosure investors are not interested in, however, is paying the amount you would get if you sold your home through normal channels, allowing enough time to find the right buyer. Instead, they are looking for rock-bottom deals—that's why they search the foreclosure notices. If you do decide to deal with these "investors," at least make several of them bid against each other for the deal that is most in your favor. This shouldn't be too difficult: Some homeowners report being contacted by sixty-five or more interested buyers when they went through foreclosure proceedings. Try to at least split the equity with them; don't just sign the house over and walk away with nothing. No matter what they say, you are not as desperate as they might wish or try to convince you that you are. As long as you own the house, you have the right to settle for nothing less than a fair deal.

20 Deal with Collection Agencies

What to say, what not to say

Collection departments and agencies get paid to do one thing: Get money from debtors. They don't care about other people's troubles or how much they cry on the phone. They are trained to ignore people's stories of woe, and may only pretend to be sympathetic when they can use it to their own advantage. They hear so many stories every day that no one can possibly tell them one they haven't heard before, and they've been lied to so many times that they probably don't believe you, either. When bill collectors sometimes get nasty and unpleasant, remember, they work every day in a world where broken promises are the norm, and every case they get represents a creditor/debtor relationship gone bad. It's no wonder that they so often bypass social niceties or that some of them seem to have been born angry.

That's not your fault, however. You don't have to take verbal lashings or tell your life story to bill collectors. You treat people with respect, and you can insist on being treated with respect, too. The best way to get respect from debt collectors is to arm yourself with knowledge. The more you know about how the debt collection system works, what you should and should not do, and your rights as a debtor, the more trouble and even anguish you can save yourself.

Call creditors before they send your account to a collection agency

Who would you rather talk to: a collection agency barracuda or a customer service representative from the company you do business with? The original creditor usually has more motivation to be civil and to try to work something out with you; the collection agency is used to getting results the hard way. The best way to deal with collection agencies is to avoid letting your debt go to them in the first place. Your creditors will usually warn you before they send a bill to collection, and they will usually delay sending it if you contact them and tell them that you are making a good faith effort to pay.

Creditors are actually reluctant to send overdue bills to collection agencies. By sending a bill to an agency, they are automatically reducing the amount they will get paid, because the agency keeps half of whatever you pay on the bill—sometimes more. They would much rather accept less than a full payment from you in most cases, or a delayed payment.

As soon as you know that you will not be able to make a minimum bill payment on time, call or write to your creditor and explain the situation. Say you cannot make the payment on time and explain why. Be brief; for example, say, "I was unemployed for two months, but I expect to receive a paycheck from my new job on the thirty-first of the month" (if that is true.) Be realistic; don't make promises that you cannot keep.

If the creditor agrees to new terms or delayed payment, be sure to get it in writing.

When they call

Find out who is calling

When the phone rings and it's a bill collector, always ask who is calling and on whose behalf. Believe it or not, many collectors call demanding payment without telling you who they really are or who they represent. I recently had a client who was repeatedly harassed by a collector who never bothered to say what the bill was for. It turned out to be for an erroneous cable bill. The man was getting calls every day about a $52 bill that was wrong. It's a lot easier to clear things up when you know the facts.

Know your rights

According to the Fair Trade Commission (FTC), you have certain rights when you are dealing with creditor and collection agencies. These include:

- **Freedom from harassment or abuse.** Collectors cannot threaten you with physical violence, call you at all hours of the night, use obscene language, or say they will publish your debts where everyone can see them.

- **Truthfulness.** Collectors cannot lie to collect debts. For example, they cannot say they are from the government or a credit bureau. They can't imply you have committed a crime. Nor can they imply they will take any legal steps, such as wage garnishment or lawsuits, that they do not intend to take. They can't send anything that looks like it comes from a government agency or an attorney's office when in fact it does not. They can't scare you by saying that you will be arrested if you do not pay.

- **Fair business practices.** The law requires collection agencies to use fair business practices. If you send them a postdated check (which is not recommended), they can't deposit it prematurely. They can't make you pay for collect phone calls. They can't violate your privacy—for example, by writing to you on a postcard. They can't make you spend extra money by wiring them money or sending a check by overnight mail. In some states, they cannot collect an amount greater than your debt.

What to tell them; what not to tell them

When debt collectors call, never forget that you have the ultimate weapon of defense: hanging up. You don't have to talk to them, even if they tell you you do. The only thing you really want out of these callers is a chance to tell them never to call again and to send you something in writing. You want them to mail you something so you can get their name and address.

Never tell debt collectors where you work, how much you make, what bank you use, or any of your relatives' names. Never tell them your checking account number, your Visa or MasterCard number, your Social Security number, or your mother's maiden name. Unfortunately, some people divulge such information when they are under enough pressure.

Don't make promises that you shouldn't. Don't let them talk you into paying more than you can afford so you then fall behind on the rent and the car payments, or miss work because you didn't save enough money out for gas. In chapter 11, you made a prioritized list of the bills you need to pay. Don't let a lower-priority bill bump a Priority 1 bill just because someone called and convinced you her bill was more important.

If you're having trouble paying your bills, never agree to automatic electronic payments from your checking account. It's far too dangerous to have money coming out of your account when you don't have a financial cushion. You will pay the bills when you get enough money.

When you are negotiating or offering to make a payment, ask a debt collector to remove any negative information from your credit report. Like everything else, get it in writing *before* you pay anything.

Some experts recommend trying to negotiate with bill collectors at the end of the month. They may be anxious to fill their quotas for the month and be willing to give you a better deal.

Tape the call if you can

If your state allows it and you are getting many calls from collection agencies, you might want to invest in a tape recorder. Most people are on their best behavior when they know a tape recorder is running. If they're not on their best behavior, at least you'll have a record of it. Before you start taping, however, find out what the law requires in your state. In some states, you can tape-record a phone conversation without telling the other party; in others you must tell the other party first. It's probably a good idea to tell people anyway. They'll be a lot more pleasant if you do.

Take notes of the call

Take good notes, whether or not you tape the conversation. Keep track of who called and when, and what was said. For one thing, if you decide later to file a complaint of harassment, you'll need more information than "He called all the time." For another thing, if the caller makes any offers or agreements, you want a record of them. Be sure to get the first and last name of the caller. Don't talk to anyone who won't tell you his or her full name.

Also ask the caller to send you something in writing. If someone promises to reduce your debt if you pay a certain amount, wait until you get that in writing before you send a cent. You can also send a letter to the debt collector with any payment agreement made over the phone. Keep a copy, and send the letter via certified mail, receipt required. That way, you can prove you sent the letter and the collector received it.

Common questions and statements made by collectors, and how to respond

Bill collectors have some really good lines. They'd be entertaining if they weren't so devious, mean-spirited, and sometimes illegal. Here are some sample lines and how you should respond:

- **"How would you like to pay this bill today?"** This collector is hoping you'll give him your bank account number or let him put the bill on another credit card. Don't you dare. Tell him, "That won't be possible." End of discussion.

- **"If you pay 50% today, you won't have to pay the rest."** Ask him to make you an offer in writing, if you're interested. Consider counteroffering with less.

- **(Loud sigh) "You're such a deadbeat. How do you live with yourself?"** Hang up. Gently. You are completely within your rights to terminate any call at any time.

- **"I'm telling your boss about this if you don't pay within ten days."** Tell him that's illegal and you know that he knows it. By law, collection agencies must keep your information private. They cannot discuss your case with anyone else—not your boss, your roommate, or even your parents (if you are over age eighteen).

- **"Where do you work?"** Say, "I'd rather not discuss that." Never tell them where you work or give them your work phone number.

- **"How much do you make?"** Again, "I don't discuss that." That's none of their business.

- **"If you pay right now, the sheriff won't come to your office next Monday."** This is pure bluff. Tell the collector to send you something in writing and never call you again. When you get the address, report the collector to the Federal Trade Commission and your state attorney general's office.

- **"I won't report anything to the credit bureau if you pay now."** If it's gone to a collection agency, it's probably already on your credit report. Tell him to send the promise in writing, and check your credit report.

- **"I can call you as often as I want, any time I want. You can't stop me."** Actually, you can stop them. Tell them not to call you again, but to send you something in writing instead. When you have their address, write to them and tell them not to contact you by phone again. They must comply. If they call you at work and you tell them that your boss does not approve of such calls, they must not call you there again.

- **(Sounding friendly and sympathetic) "How did you get so far behind in your bills?"** Don't tell your life story. Don't say anything about why you lost your job, your bad-news boyfriend, your carpal tunnel syndrome, or how you've just been so stressed out lately. It won't do any good and it's none of their business. They can turn on you at any minute and use the information you just gave them to make you feel even worse or to take other measures. The answer to this question is "That's not the point." Period.

Always stay calm, or at least sound like you're calm, when you are talking to a collector. Keep an attitude of looking for a solution to the problem, and never let them know that they are getting to you.

I got them to stop calling. Now what?

If you send collectors a letter telling them not to call you on the phone or otherwise contact you, they cannot contact you again except to tell you that they received your letter and will not be contacting you further, or when they intend to take further action. If you actually owe the money, however, the debt does not go away. The collector can go through legal processes, such as suing you to recover the amount you owe.

When you send a payment for less than the full amount, if that is what was agreed on, you can write "Payment in Full" on the check. However, you must also have the agreement in writing from the collector. By itself, cashing a check that has "Payment in Full" written on it does not legally bind the collector to accepting it as final settlement.

What if I don't believe I owe the money?

If you get a call or a letter from a collection agency or a creditor and you don't believe that you owe the money, *never* ignore it. If you don't contest the bill within thirty days, the collector can assume that it is valid. Immediately respond with a letter stating why you do not believe you owe the money.

Report collection violations

Report any violations by collection agencies and creditors to the Federal Trade Commission (FTC) and the attorney general's office in your state.

Like most other laws, debt collection laws vary by state. For more information, contact the attorney general's office. You can usually find the Web site of the attorney general by typing "attorney general" and the name of your state into an Internet search engine.

You can get more information about how the FTC can help you, or file a complaint, on the Internet at http://www.ftc.gov/bcp/con line/edcams/credit/index.html or by calling toll-free 1-877-FTC-HELP (1-877-382-4357).

You can also get a free consumer brochure called *What You Should Know About Debt Collection* from the National Consumer Law Center by calling 617-542-9595.

21 Stay Sane

*You're still you, and
they can't change that*

Financial problems are more than stressful. They can be humiliating. In a society that seems to measure success in dollars, financial problems can make debtors feel like their self-worth is as low as their bank accounts. We know better. We know that financial net worth has absolutely nothing to do with someone's worth as a person. We just need to be reminded sometimes.

It helps to remember that some of the most respected and influential people in history have endured tough financial times. For example:

A poor boy from Missouri became a world-famous writer. He married a girl from a wealthy family, and they had three girls of their own. They lived in a beautiful house and had it all—trips to Europe, fancy bicycles, maids—until he made some truly disastrous investments. People wondered how such a smart man could make such bad business decisions. What hurt him most was that he not only lost his fortune, he even lost his wife's inheritance. There seemed to be no way that he could make enough money to recoup his losses. In an era when travel was still difficult and dangerous, he packed up and made an around-the-world speaking tour to pay off his debts and get back on his feet financially. Who was he? Samuel Clemens (pen name Mark Twain).

A clever boy from a modest family background was dismissed from school and called "hopeless" by his teacher. From then on, his mother taught him herself. He rose to wealth and fame with his ingenuity and inventiveness. However, he wasn't afraid to try things that might fail—and his new concrete factory failed spectacularly! It lost millions of dollars and went bankrupt twice. He lost everything, and his concrete furniture idea became a laughing-stock. He had to start over, but his "1% inspiration, 99% perspiration" formula served him well. Thomas Edison went on to become a legendary investor and businessman.

Perhaps the most famous figure with money woes was once a motherless child in the American wilderness. His family lived through one winter in something that couldn't really be called a log cabin; it was just a lean-to that he couldn't even stand up in. He educated himself and went into business—where he failed not just once but repeatedly. He married a woman from a prominent family who was used to spending money on whatever she wanted, and she continued to spend money faster than he could ever make it. One of the first things he was really successful at was becoming president of the United States, and he remains one of the most loved and respected figures of all time. He was Abraham Lincoln.

Clemens, Edison, and Lincoln all experienced financial successes and failures. Because of their perserverance, they left us a legacy far more valuable than money. You can think of other examples, perhaps in your own family or in your hometown. By looking at the lives of other people who have survived tough times, you can gain confidence that you can make it, too.

Avoid negative thinking

It's easy to say, "Think positive!" It's much harder to stay positive when you're under financial strain day after day. You can, however, change your thinking patterns to more constructive ones so you are more likely to succeed and to be happier on the road to success.

I'm not going to ask you to visualize wealth coming your way, or to dwell on what you'll do with all that money once it gets here. In fact, I'd rather you didn't. Visualizing ways to spend money when you're trying to save it makes as much sense as drooling at the window of a Danish bakery while you're trying to lose weight. Improving your financial situation takes hard work, and you might not see results overnight.

Instead, look at some of the ways you think about money and about people who have it or don't, and decide whether you need to change your thought patterns.

Don't think more or less of people because of how much money they have

Most of us do realize that our worth is not dependent on how much money we have—but do we treat other people differently depending on how well-off they are? If we do, then in our hearts we know we are hypocrites. If we forgive someone for being a jerk because she has a yacht, or if we go out to eat with a pompous bore because he always picks up the tab, then we really do value people based on what they own, not who they are. If our heroes are all rich, if we admire people more for making and spending money than for how they help other people, our values are not what we claim.

How can we expect other people, let alone our inner selves, to value *us* as human beings irrespective of our financial status if we respect the rich just because they're rich and snub people who have less?

On the other hand, don't fall into the trap of thinking less of people just because they *do* have money. That's called envy, and it is nothing but destructive. If you don't like financially successful people, if you think people are better just because they're poor, you might even subconsciously sabotage yourself to keep from becoming one of those hated "rich people"! Value people because they are human beings. Admire them for their character, their personality, and their talents. Money has nothing to do with what they—or you—are worth.

Don't let your background tell you who you are

Many people see themselves as deserving about what they grew up with. They might hope to do a little better, but they expect to stay in the same economic class all their life. Somehow, the daughter of a successful professional couple naturally sees herself going through college, reaching one goal at a time, and having a certain standard of living as an adult. If she has older brothers and sisters in school ahead of her, the path may seem preplanned—even expected.

The daughter of a family with less education and fewer resources, however, can fall into the trap of thinking she is the kind of person who will always have less money. It's in her genes. It's the way people in her family are. People who buy nice houses and have nice things are "other people," not her.

It's hard to shake the financial image of yourself that you grow up with. You can be whoever you want to be, though. Money doesn't prefer one person over another. Anyone can learn to earn and manage money successfully.

Other people fear being financially successful because they have seen money—or more often the pursuit of money—misused. If their parents were so busy trying to make money that they never had time to play with their children, or if every dinner-table conversation seemed to revolve around making or saving money, they may be repulsed by talk about money. If a child grows up in a home where Dad calculates the cost of the glass of orange juice she's holding, she may see budgeting as mean and distasteful. Maybe someone's parents talked down people who had more money; in that case, why would he want to join a group that his parents despised?

Remember why you want to be in control of your money

Life is much more than money, but when your money is out of control, your options are severely limited. Money may not be everything, but it does pay for warm homes, trips to Grandma's house, and new crayons for the kids. We make money and manage it wisely so we can take care of the people we love.

You need to be in control of your money so that your money troubles don't control your life. When you can pay your bills this month and you know how you will pay your bills next month, you will be able to focus your attention on your health, your friendships, and everything else that matters to you. That's the real goal of this book—to help you manage your money so that you can go on and live your life to the fullest, not hampered by money worries. I hope that I have helped you along that path.

Conclusion

Never give up

By the time you have read *Help! I Can't Pay My Bills,* you should know how to look realistically at your financial situation, find more money to pay your bills with, and lower your expenses and debts. You should also know how to make the best use of your money when you pay your bills. These are huge steps, and no one can say that they are easy, but these steps are absolutely essential if you want to take control of your money.

When you are in better control of your money, you will find that you need to think about money less, not more. When your finances were a disaster, they caused you stress every day. You may not have even known how bad they were, or you didn't want to know. When you know where you stand financially and where your money goes, you feel more secure.

If you don't have time to implement all the ideas in this book, find one thing you can do today to take control of your money—even if it's only to gather up the courage to look honestly at your financial situation. Read chapter 2 and choose something in the checklist that you can do or change right now. Every change, no matter how small, will help.

Changing spending habits is difficult at first, but soon it becomes a habit. As a reformed spender, you may find it hard to believe how much money was slipping away before you mended your ways. You may even look at people around you and cringe at the way they part with their money so easily when they get so little in return. You may have to stop looking at other people's grocery carts—it's too appalling to see how they can fill up their carts with expensive boxes that contain precious little real food. Like a reformed smoker, you can't believe that people live the way that you may have lived, not so long ago.

Celebrate every success as you learn to manage your money more effectively. Financial success is not about getting rich. It's about no longer feeling like a victim struggling daily to survive financially, but instead being in charge of your money and your future. You can make it. You can control your finances—and your life.

Index